For Rick:

The Second Wind
is for you!

Luke
1:57

"For those banged and bruised by life's first half, for those struggling with who to be and what to do with the thirty 'bonus years' twenty-first century people are given, *Second Wind* is a book of hope and promise."

—BOB BUFORD, founder of Leadership Network and author of
Halftime: Changing Your Game Plan from Success to Significance

"Bill Butterworth makes me laugh, but even more important, he makes me think. Bill is much more than an inspirational speaker, more than a teacher. He is a locomotive of energy, commitment, and faith in our Judeo-Christian principles. No wonder I like him so much."

—JACK KEMP, former congressman and codirector of Empower
America

SECOND WIND

THE PROMISE OF THE SECOND WIND

IT'S NEVER TOO LATE *to* PURSUE GOD'S BEST

BILL BUTTERWORTH & DEAN MERRILL

WATERBROOK
PRESS

SECOND WIND
PUBLISHED BY WATERBROOK PRESS
2375 Telstar Drive, Suite 160
Colorado Springs, Colorado 80920
A division of Random House, Inc.

ISBN 1-57856-761-0

Published in association with the literary agency of Alive Communications, Inc., 7680 Goddard Street, Suite 200, Colorado Springs, CO 80920.

Library of Congress Cataloging-in-Publication Data
Butterworth, Bill.
   The promise of the second wind : it's never too late to pursue God's best / Bill Butterworth and Dean Merrill.—1st ed.
      p. cm.
Includes bibliographical references.
   ISBN 1-57856-761-0
   1. Self-actualization (Psychology)—Religious aspects—Christianity. 2. Consolation. 3. Loss (Psychology)—Religious aspects—Christianity. 4. Life change events—Religious aspects—Christianity. 5. Christian life. I. Merrill, Dean. II. Title.
   BV4598.2.B88 2003
   248.8'4—dc21

2003013621

Printed in the United States of America
2003—First Edition

10 9 8 7 6 5 4 3 2 1

For Kathi

You are God's beautiful seashell I discovered
as I was running the beach of life.

Thanks for handing me the lapel mike.

–Bill

CONTENTS

Foreword

You are holding *hope* in your hands, because this life-changing book is brimming with heartfelt encouragement, godly guidance, and helpful support.

My friends Bill Butterworth and Dean Merrill assure us that when we are in the midst of financial despair, relational chaos, medical fears, or spiritual confusion, there still remains the promise of the Second Wind. It's a message we all need to hear.

I've known the cool, refreshing breeze of the Second Wind at pivotal moments in my own life. When I was parched spiritually, mired in a world of atheism, God offered yet another chance for me to meet him personally. When sickness came, when I almost trashed my marriage, when financial pressures were mounting, I found there was still hope through the God of the second chance.

I can remember poignantly when my purpose in life seemed hopelessly muddled. I was a successful newspaper editor and new Christian at the time. But after nearly fourteen years in journalism, my life started to feel stale and predictable. I was making a good living and serving the community through journalism, but I was developing a strong desire to invest the best hours of my day directly in God's work.

An opportunity arose for me to leave journalism and enter into the ministry at a thriving and cutting-edge church. The move was fraught with uncertainty. My income would be cut in half. Could we still afford to pay the mortgage? How would we put our children through school? My training was in journalism and law. Would I really be able to provide the kind of help that people need in their spiritual journeys?

Despite my hesitancy, my wife, Leslie, and I moved ahead in our new adventure, our sails billowing with God's Second Wind. He not only carried us through the difficult times, but he created new opportunities for me to return to writing. As a journalist my contribution had morphed into an editing and managerial role; now, however, I was able to use my once-dormant writing skills to tell millions of people about Jesus Christ. Nothing has been more satisfying than that!

You'll read lots of other true stories in this inspiring and motivating book. You'll meet real people who are dealing with real struggles in a very real and often scary world. Just when we think God's response might be the harsh gale of cold condemnation, instead he graciously sends the loving whisper of his Second Wind, enabling quite ordinary people to achieve very extraordinary results.

Wherever you are in your own spiritual journey—confused about God or an enthusiastic follower of his—you will find hope and help in this powerful volume. In fact, the Bible says our hope is anchored in the resurrection of Jesus of Nazareth, the history-shattering event that proved once and for all that he has the power to overcome death.

Because he lives, because he has the supernatural power of God, and because he cares deeply about you personally, the Second Wind will always be blowing. Read this important book, and you'll learn how you can let that breeze carry you deeper and deeper into God's exciting purpose for your life.

—LEE STROBEL
author, *The Case for Christ*

Acknowledgments

The older I get, the more I realize the value in the friendships I have shared. Many of them were significant in the telling of this story. Some in big ways, some in small, but all important.

Dean Merrill is the consummate professional. I am so fortunate to have his name next to mine on this book's cover. Behind that wild and crazy exterior is a very serious writer!

I am grateful to my friends at Alive Communications for helping me put this project together. I am especially thankful to *Lee Hough* for his help and insight.

The folks at WaterBrook Press are wonderful. *Bruce Nygren* provided careful editorial assistance, and I am very thankful for a deepening friendship with my publisher, *Don Pape*.

God brought some excellent writers into my life, not only as friends, but as men to prod me on to higher goals. *Lee Strobel* has become one of my dearest friends and a constant encourager. *Ken Gire* was very instrumental in the birth of this project and has believed in me for almost twenty years now. *Steve Arterburn* can always brighten my day with a humorous thought or an amazing new idea.

There are other friends who have been in my corner for the long haul. *Joe and Molly Davis, Mike and Marcia Scott, Ron and Kay Nelson, Bob and Barb Ludwig, Ken and Mari Harrower, Gary and Linda Bender, Al and Anita Manley* are all so important to me in vital ways.

I've been blessed to speak in front of some amazing churches. Some of my favorite people are pastors. I so appreciate *Bill Hybels, Rick Warren, Stu Boehmig, Ray Johnston, Gene Appel, Kenton Beshore* and *Randy Frazee*, just to name a few.

I've met other outstanding guys over the years through corporate speaking. Just like their pastoral counterparts, these men have provided me hours of encouragement along my journey. I am grateful for buddies like *Bill Morton, Mark Zoradi, Mike Sime, Mike Regan,* and *Robert Kulhawy.*

Beyond the scope of friendship, I have a family beyond my wildest dreams. I thank God every day for my daughter, *Joy,* her husband, *Justin,* my little granddaughter, *Jill,* my son *Jesse,* his wife, *Marisa,* my sons, *Jeffrey, John, and Joseph.* They are my crowning achievement.

My wife, *Kathi,* is the gift of sweetest wonder. She has lovingly watched me experience my Second Wind and has been at my side all the way. She is more than I could have ever dreamed of.

Thank you, *dear Lord,* for teaching me about the Second Wind.

WHO'S TALKING?

As you may have already figured out, the previous acknowledgments were written by Bill Butterworth. In a book such as this with a two-person byline, some parts are from Bill, others from Dean. Especially when we tell personal stories, we need to identify who is the "I" in the narrative.

That's why you'll find our names sprinkled throughout the chapters. They will clearly indicate whose voice is speaking in the passage.

However, many sections will be unmarked, because we've truly collaborated on the content. It is the product of both minds coming together to express the promise of the Second Wind to you.

We hope this guides your understanding as you read.

Huffing Toward Forty-Fourth Street

—Bill—

Like about sixty-seven million other people my age and weight, I'm going to get back in shape. I really am. Don't laugh. I'm serious about this.

In fact, I've begun a new daily routine. I live near the ocean, and so at some point each day that I'm not traveling, I make my way over to the beach and…

I RUN.

Maybe that's a little strong. Actually, I run.

Of course, if you really press me, I'd have to say I run/walk.

Or, more accurately, I run/WALK.

Okay, I WALK.

But lately I've been making headway. I honestly have been moving from a brisk walk to a solid jog during more and more portions of my beach journey. I run close to the water, where the sand is wet and thus more solid. It's easier on my massive hulk than slogging through loose sand, and it's a natural progression from the first part of my trek.

The first thing I do when I hit the beach is search for the prettiest seashell I can find. I hold it in my hand; it helps me focus on the reasons

I'm hoofing through the sand. It also helps me zero in on a particular prayer request that I bring before the Lord each day as I'm running.

One day it might be something about one of my five children. Another day it's a vocational issue. Sometimes I pray for my wife or for a particular aspect of my own life. That shell is the closest this lifelong Protestant will ever get to a set of rosary beads. Just the simple act of handling it holds my attention on the request.

Another reason I find a seashell is that it reminds me that despite the pain I feel during this beach run, there's still something of beauty to be taken from it. It's kind of "stop and smell the roses," only at the beach. When I get back home, I add the shell to a lovely glass container on my desk. As the glass fills up, I am further inspired to keep running each day.

HITTING THE WALL

That's the fun part. Now let's get back to the rest of my reality.

I hate to run. Always have. Probably always will. I've struggled with extra poundage my entire life. I have no ambition to do a marathon, join a jogging club, or qualify as a poster boy for zero percent body fat.

A typical journey finds me briskly walking the beach as far as a certain pier, about thirty-five to forty minutes away. I touch one of the pilings there, then turn back and head toward home, running as I go.

It's not pretty. I huff and puff. Passersby give me a look that says, *That guy could be making his final run!* I pant. I sweat. The longer I run, the more pain I feel. First it's localized in my legs and lungs. Soon the pain invades my head, my arms, my stomach, my feet. If I concentrate hard enough, I think I can feel my eyebrows hurt.

Things start happening mentally. *You'd better stop,* my brain says to me, first subtly, then screaming. *You'll feel so much better walking. It's more comfortable. It makes better sense.*

When I first began this regimen, I would listen to my brain and quit running. But then I arrived home feeling deflated, discouraged, and defeated.

So I made myself a goal that I would run just a little farther down the beach each day. You know—baby steps.

That idea worked for a while, but I would hit the wall at a particular point that was brutal. The city even erected a monument, memorializing where my pain was most deeply felt…

It was the lifeguard stand at Forty-fourth Street.

I grew to despise that lifeguard stand. The sight of its two fours painted next to each other on the side of the large wooden hut sickened me. *I'm not sure I'm cut out for this,* I started telling myself. *Think back to all the fun of parking in the old recliner with a dozen donuts and a tub of ice cream.*

My brain really knows how to get to my brain. It almost had its way with me. I almost quit.

And then it happened.

One day as I kicked the pier piling and started running homeward, I got to the Forty-fourth Street lifeguard stand—and something inside urged me to push on. For some reason I listened to that voice and kept running. As I continued, the strangest sensation swept through my system. I was suddenly reenergized, as if I had tapped into a new wellspring of power. Something inside of me felt as if it had just been connected to a set of jumper cables. I was almost swept up into a Superman feeling, except that the silhouette of my body on the beach seemed to hint that maybe Superman should consider the Atkins diet.

Anyway, with my newly discovered energy, I finished my run in a sprint of exhilaration. Triumphantly arriving at my finish line, I threw my fists into the air like Rocky Balboa atop the steps of the Philadelphia Museum of Art. Fortunately nobody on the beach knew me; people just stared at me in silence.

But it didn't matter to me.

Something wonderful had happened.

I had experienced a *second wind.*

LONGING FOR A FRESH START

—Dean—

This is not a book about running. It's a book about the need for a second wind in life and where to find it.

The longer you live, the greater your chances of running out of steam. Call it fatigue, call it disappointment, call it bad luck…the energy just isn't there anymore. People wake up one day and realize they're just plodding through life and feeling stuck. They're weary with the sameness of day in, day out. They had hoped for better things, a more exciting life, a higher level of accomplishment—but instead they have settled for what is rather than what could have been.

Here are three examples I know. I've changed the names and circumstances so as not to cause problems for the individuals involved, but the feelings are authentic and real.

TOM

He backs his six-year-old Ford Taurus out of the driveway and heads for the boulevard once again, the same route to work he has taken ten thousand times. He is not happy this cloudy Thursday morning, not because anything particularly terrible has happened, but because nothing particularly exciting is in store either. Not today, not tomorrow, not the upcoming weekend, not ever.

He will spend another day at his Department of Motor Vehicles desk, watching over his team of eight clerks at the windows as they issue license plates, process title applications, and collect fees that inevitably irritate the public. Every hour or so he will be called over to settle a dispute, to calm down a citizen who's sure he's being robbed by a greedy government. In between these skirmishes, he fills out paperwork, writes reports, and monitors efficiency.

It's not a bad job. Somebody has to do it, and every other Friday it produces a paycheck to keep his family afloat. What eats at his forty-nine-year-old soul, however, is that with his modest qualifications, his lack of a college diploma, and his hesitancy to take any kind of risk or make a splash, this is basically all there's going to be. His name isn't going to show up in the promotion announcements that get e-mailed to everyone from time to time. He's a cog in the great wheel of bureaucracy, turning, turning, turning each day, unnoticed and unheralded.

Over his brown-bag lunch at noon, Tom thinks about his wife, surrounded in her classroom by twenty-eight fresh-faced third graders. They're noisy at times, but they're eager to learn, and they think their teacher is a wonder woman. He muses…*Well, the kids are right; she is terrific at what she does. She turns them on to a marvelous world. She's really made something of herself. She sparks excitement, and she draws energy in return.*

This he finds depressing in an odd sort of way, because he wonders what she really thinks down deep inside about her gray, paper-shuffling, dead-ended husband. He does not worry about her turning from their marriage; she's much too principled for that. But she yearns for a nicer house in a better neighborhood, something that only a higher salary could bring—and that's not going to happen. Their high school freshman son wants to play hockey, but the gear is awfully expensive. Their computer in the family room keeps crashing for some reason, and he doesn't know how to fix it…

Sweeping his potato chip remnants and sandwich bag toward the trash can, Tom stares into space, wondering.

SUSAN

She glances toward the scratched-up door of her modest apartment as she hears the familiar Sunday evening noise. Her boys are clambering up the steps, back from another weekend with their father. Now she must get their feet back on the ground to be ready for school in the morning. Since the divorce three years ago, her world has quivered like a flawed gyroscope, but she's hanging on, determined to make the best of a rough ride.

"Hi, guys," she greets them. "Did you have a good time?"

"Oh, Mom, it was so cool!" exudes the younger one. "Dad took us to this paintball place, and we all put on these other clothes so we could blast each other with red and green and purple and every color you can imagine. I got Jeremy once right in the face—it was awesome!"

She forces a smile as she tousles her son's hair and nudges him down the hall, dragging his duffel bag, toward the bedroom the two boys must share. There she sorts out what goes straight into the laundry while simultaneously asking whether any homework for tomorrow still remains undone. Next will come showers for both of them and, soon enough, bedtime.

This isn't the life Susan dreamed of, to be sure. Clenching her jaw, she manages each challenge as it comes, pushing down her feelings into the basement of her mind so she can concentrate on the immediate. The boys don't seem to be all that much worse for the wear, although she can't tell for sure what's happening at school. Last week a teacher's note had come home saying, "Be sure to call for an appointment with me during Parents' Week, okay?" What would that be about?

The next morning will start with an early rush, and so she lays out her clothes tonight for the coming workday. Finally she sags into bed, makes sure the alarm is set for 5:40, and then reaches for the Bible on her night-stand. Finding her bookmark from the last time, she picks up the trail again with Isaiah. The Edomite nation has done something wrong—she's not quite sure what—and they're now going to get it from an angry God whose patience has been used up. She keeps plodding along to the next chapter, but the dark tone persists. She was hoping for some lift, some encourage-ment from Scripture, but, oh well... Susan closes the book with a sigh and turns out the light.

BRAD

He turns on his computer on a Friday morning, and up pops a meeting request. George, his boss, wants to see him at three o'clock. Topic: un-stated.

It strikes him as odd, because he's already had his weekly update ses-sion with George at the normal time on Wednesday morning. *What's up?* he wonders.

Anyway, he clicks the Accept Appointment button and moves on to other work. But throughout the day, he keeps guessing to himself. Is George going to retire? Has corporate headquarters sent down a new proj-ect? Is there a merger in the wind?

The day drags by slowly, until finally three o'clock arrives. He walks into George's office to find a coworker already there. And quickly a third member of the team arrives. Both of the others look as puzzled as he does.

George is unusually agitated. He keeps twisting a pencil in his right hand. "Go ahead and close the door," he says with a nod.

And within twenty minutes all three managers have been told they're out of work. The company's earnings in the past two quarters have slipped to the point that Wall Street has noticed, the firm's bond rating has dropped, and an alarmed board of directors has now mandated a 12 percent reduction in work force.

"I am terribly sorry, guys," George concludes. "This is definitely not your fault. You've worked very hard and given your best to this company. But I have no choice; the brass says I've got to cut somewhere, and this is how I've decided to do it."

The trio ask more questions about severance procedures, of course. But all too soon the meeting is over.

Brad shuffles back to his office, his mind in a blur. Now what? He picks up his phone to call his wife. "Honey, are you there? I just wanted to make sure. I'm coming home early."

"Yes, okay… Um, what's happening?" she wants to know.

"Well, I'll tell you when I get there."

"No, really. Something's wrong. I can hear it in your voice," she insists. "Tell me now."

He sucks in a breath and then says, "Um…the company is not making its numbers these days, and…I just got laid off."

"Oh no!" she exclaims. "How can they do this to you, after all the hours you've put in and everything?!" She sniffs, trying to choke back the tears.

Finally she says, "Hurry home right away… I love you." With that, they hang up, and Brad reaches for his coat.

The Promise Waits for You

—Bill—

These slices of life, and dozens of others, can be positively affected by the promise of the Second Wind. It can happen—it can happen to you.

This is a book of hope. It's a book for the weary. It's for those who looked at its title and found it almost too upbeat. It's for those at the Forty-fourth Street lifeguard stand of life who aren't sure they can make it home again.

I know that forsaken feeling. I know what it feels like to be fresh out of fuel. I went through a divorce several years ago that left me a lifeless lump. Energy escaped me. Life seemed to leave. Each day was nothing more than a twenty-four-hour sigh.

But I have good news.

I've experienced a rejuvenation in my life. I'll tell you more about it as we move through the book. But trust me, it has jump-started my life again.

Yes, I have been honored as a recipient of the coveted Second Wind. And I've sneaked a peek at this year's recipients...

You're on the list.

Personal Journal

- Based on Bill's story of jogging on the beach, how would you describe a second wind in the runner's world?

_____

_____

_____

_____

_____

_____

- How does that translate into life? What does a Second Wind in the everyday world look like to you?

_____

_____

_____

_____

_____

- What prompted you to read this book? Are you looking for a Second Wind? What will it look like to you?

_____

_____

_____

_____

_____

- What are the current circumstances of your life that put you in the position of desiring a Second Wind? Describe them.

_____

_____

_____

_____

_____

_____

- Can you relate to any of the three vignettes that were included in this chapter? The DMV employee? The single mom? The man who lost his job? Being as specific as you can, what is it about these stories that causes you to empathize with them?

_____

_____

_____

_____

_____

_____

- Read Psalm 42 slowly and thoughtfully. Jot down keywords and key phrases that speak to you in the text.

Verse   _Keyword or Key Phrase_

_____

_____

_____

_____

_____

_____

_____

- Spend some time in prayer. Tell God about your life and thank him for his promise of the Second Wind for you. Ask him to bring that Second Wind into your life in his own timing, in his own way.

In the Midst
of the Ordinary

—Bill—

"Okay, guys, let's spend a little time looking at Philippians 2," says the brown-haired man with the glasses at the end of the table, pushing back his coffee mug to make room for his Bible. That's the signal of Charlie Spicer, moderator of our Friday morning men's group, that we need to transition from casual jokes and football talk to some spiritual food.

A successful sales executive with a men's apparel company, Charlie's the kind of guy whom friends and customers naturally trust. He doesn't badger, overpromise, or manipulate. He just shows the connection between his product and your need, allowing you to draw your own conclusion. It's a trait that runs deep in the Spicer genes; Charlie's father and grandfather before him were both salesmen in the paper industry, and it was only natural for the grandson to take up the same line of work.

His first employer, NCR, spotted his potential early on and tapped him for a management development program, eventually paying for his MBA degree. Awards and plaques began to collect around Charlie's desk. Salesman of the Year, among others. He sold for Mead Paper Company awhile, then moved into marketing high-tech software.

"I like selling," he says. "For one thing, you can make good money. I also like the flexibility of schedule; I'm not chained behind a desk all day. Instead, I'm out and about in a car, calling on customers, setting my own pace."

A third factor that has always meant something to Charlie is the chance to meet a lot of people and help them. The human contact is a reward of its own.

As a result, his wife, Denise, and their two daughters enjoy a comfortable lifestyle in the Orange County suburbs of Los Angeles. Life is good. Not spectacular, not dramatic. Just okay.

And that's the part that's been nagging at Charlie the last few years. He's been asking God if, here at age forty, there could be any way to find more meaning in his work.

"I first began to take God seriously as a result of the birth of our first daughter back in 1991," Charlie says. "Watching this new little life come into the world really spoke to me. I started to think, *I have a family now. I need to be a leader in my home, and I don't know how to do that. I need to get my act together, don't I?*

Soon Charlie and Denise discovered a church in their community with a Tuesday night family life group. They found themselves sitting around tables discussing how to be better parents and how God's strength could make a difference. "The whole idea of being 'born again'—I took it very literally," says Charlie. "For me, it was a chance to grow up again. Only this time, I had the Holy Spirit to guide my steps."

What If...?

As time went on, the Spicers progressed to become table leaders, and their spiritual knowledge deepened. Sitting and talking with a younger couple and showing them how to put the Lord at the center of their marriage and parenting brought more and more fulfillment. People seemed to flower under their mentoring.

The church asked them to work especially with engaged couples, getting them ready for a lifetime commitment. One evening in early 2002, after a dinner appointment with a couple that had gone especially well, they were driving home when Denise said with all seriousness, "Charlie, what if you did this for a living? You did so great tonight; you were gentle and kind, and yet you helped guide them and answer their questions." There were tears in her eyes as she looked across at her husband.

Charlie stared ahead at the traffic. It was not a brand-new thought; he had privately fantasized about being a pastor someday. But his wife's comment brought the whole crazy notion forward in a new way.

"Yes, I would really enjoy that," he answered. "But how in the world would we ever pull it off? I'd have to go back to school, that's for sure. I'm not qualified to be a counselor or whatever. I don't know…"

They were both pensive, drawn toward the new but reluctant to jettison the old. As they pulled into the driveway, Denise said, "Why don't you at least explore the possibilities?" Charlie nodded. It took both of them awhile to go to sleep that night.

In the weeks that followed, Charlie began making phone calls and checking Web sites to learn more about training options. What would it really take to become a credentialed MFT, as they called it—a marriage-and-family therapist? He studied the course offerings of several graduate schools. He calculated how much of the work could be done through night classes, after his day job was completed.

When he looked at the tuition costs, however, his pragmatic self took over. *Who am I kidding?* he said to himself. *With the mortgage and all the other bills we already have, there's no way I can do this. Get real, man.*

The dream seemed hazy indeed. Starting a whole new career in midlife was fun to imagine, but it was also highly unrealistic.

DAY IN, DAY OUT

The more bits and pieces of Charlie's thinking I heard on Friday mornings, the more I thought about Moses in the Old Testament. Here was a man who had spent forty years taking care of sheep in the desert, doing the same-old same-old every day, every week, every season…until God showed up unexpectedly with a fresh new idea for his life.

For a CliffsNotes biography of this man, see the way Stephen retold it in just eighteen verses of Acts 7. It starts in verse 20:

> At that time Moses was born, and he was no ordinary child. For
> three months he was cared for in his parents' home. When he was
> placed outside, Pharaoh's daughter took him and brought him up
> as her own son. Moses was educated in all the wisdom of the Egyp-
> tians and was powerful in speech and action.

I suppose if you have to surrender your child to a foster home, you could do far worse than having him land in the palace! What a great break this was, under the circumstances.

The Bible says (both here and in Hebrews 11:23), "He was no ordinary child." In other words, Moses was in the gifted program. As an adult he "was powerful in speech and action" (Acts 7:22), despite the excuse he tried to give God later about his public-speaking ability.

However, everything went south one fateful day:

> When Moses was forty years old, he decided to visit his own people,
> the Israelites. He saw one of them being mistreated by an Egyptian,

so he went to his defense and avenged him by killing the Egyptian. Moses thought that his own people would realize that God was using him to rescue them, but they did not. The next day Moses came upon two Israelites who were fighting. He tried to reconcile them by saying, "Men, you are brothers; why do you want to hurt each other?"

But the man who was mistreating the other pushed Moses aside and said, "Who made you ruler and judge over us? Do you want to kill me as you killed the Egyptian yesterday?" When Moses heard this, he fled to Midian. (verses 23-29)

Here is a man who sees the world's pain and injustice and decides to do something about it—right now—*violently.* His emotions override his good sense. Within twenty-four hours this has spawned a whole tempest of misunderstanding. Moses soon realizes that his connections back at the palace probably aren't going to save his neck; he's guilty of homicide of a government employee.

In a panic he heads for the border. And that is how he winds up on the shelf, vocationally speaking.

He fled to Midian, where he settled as a foreigner and had two sons. After forty years had passed… (verses 29-30)

What a huge block of living is encapsulated in these few words. Can you think of anything more dull than…get up, have coffee, put on your robe, buckle your sandals, go out, hang with the sheep, have a peanut-butter-and-jelly sandwich out of a brown bag at noon, hang with the sheep all afternoon, then put them away at night, go home—and go to bed early, because tomorrow will be the same thing again. (I'm extrapolating just a bit on the menu items, I admit, but you get the point.)

Ever get a day off? No. Sheep have to be watched seven days a week. This goes on for ten years…twenty…thirty…forty.

As my kids would say, "Borrrrr-ing!"

I can imagine Moses stuffing his guilt and frustration, thinking, *I bet if anybody knew the whole story of what happened back there in Egypt, they wouldn't even trust me to watch the sheep. I'm a loser.*

If somebody had come by one day and said, "Tell me about your past, Moses," how do you think he would have replied?

"Well, I really don't want to talk about it."

"Why not?"

A pained glare and then: "You know, that's why I hang with the sheep. They don't ask a lot of questions."

Does this man have any kind of a future? Not that we can see.

Surprise in the Sinai

And then, on an ordinary day, without warning…

An angel appeared to Moses in the flames of a burning bush in the desert near Mount Sinai. When he saw this, he was amazed at the sight. As he went over to get a closer look, he heard the Lord say: "I am the God of your fathers, the God of Abraham, Isaac and Jacob." Moses trembled with fear and did not dare to look.

Then the Lord said to him, "Take off your sandals; the place where you are standing is holy ground. I have indeed seen the oppression of my people in Egypt. I have heard their groaning and have come down to set them free. Now come, I will send you back to Egypt."

This is the same Moses they had rejected with the words, "Who made you ruler and judge?" He was sent to be their ruler and deliverer by God himself, through the angel who appeared to him in the bush. (verses 30-35)

Who could have predicted this surprise encounter with God? Not one of us. God suddenly steps out of nowhere to reveal himself and unveil a whole new future for Moses. No wonder he "trembled with fear" (verse 32). You and I would too. This is a perfectly understandable reaction to the coming of God's Second Wind.

If God were ever to repeat this phenomenon, what item in your life would he choose to torch? Could there ever be…

a burning bookcase in your office?

a burning band saw in your shop?

a burning blackboard in your school?

a burning blender in your kitchen? (Actually, I've had that experience, but it wasn't any of God's doing.)

My point is this: We live in the ordinary. It's God who steps in and does the extraordinary.

God initiates, Moses responds. Moses didn't start the conversation by saying, "Jehovah, Jehovah" with God replying "Here I am." No, it was the other way around.

When Jesus came to this world, he took the initiative to say to people who were discouraged, stuck, and dead-ended, "Come to me, all you who are weary and burdened, and I will give you rest" (Matthew 11:28). It was an honest, personal invitation—not like the loads of junk mail that fill our mailboxes trying to get us to come for real estate seminars, a free massage, or landscaping for our backyards. When Jesus said, "Come," it really meant something.

When Jehovah said to Moses, "Go, and I will authenticate you," it meant the start of a whole new future for a man who had assumed he had none whatsoever.

LISTENING INWARD

Too often in life we are prone to assume that the die is already cast. Maybe there were bright options when we were teenagers or in college or in early adulthood. But not now. Our lives have become locked in, the clay has hardened, the groove has become too deep. The resulting boredom is simply the price we pay for getting older.

All of which makes no sense at all to a God who is *timeless*. He doesn't live by clocks and calendars. He operates in a whole bigger dimension.

My friend Charlie Spicer found out that Vanguard University, a Christian college right down the road from his home, had a master of science program in clinical psychology. No need to uproot his family for a cross-country move. Due to the evening scheduling, it would take him three and a half years to complete. But halfway through the program, he'd actually begin taking counseling appointments under supervision.

And when it came to cost, there was a generous student loan waiting, with a ten-year payback plan. He and Denise ran the numbers, and they worked out after all, assuming that he would keep his present job to float the family expenses.

They began to pray in earnest. *Lord, is this really what you want us to do?* The more they prayed and the more affirmations that came from the leadership of their church as well as individuals, the more they began to embrace the new dream.

Charlie took a deep breath and submitted an application. He was accepted into the program. He started classes in the fall of 2002.

Have there been misgivings? Of course—just like Moses, who questioned God more than once about his commission. Sometimes my friend frets about whether he can keep up academically with all the bright young minds around him on campus. But he says, "That's 'the old Charlie' getting nervous. The truth is, I am excited about this. I don't want to go back. My mind can't be allowed to lead me. My heart must lead, as it hears what God is saying to me.

"I'm realizing that I have to be *inward*-directed. What God speaks to my heart is more important than what people say. That sounds odd coming from a salesman, I know; we're schooled to always stay alert to the customer. But this isn't a business transaction. This is going with the wind of the Spirit."

In fact, from my perspective as Charlie's friend, I can tell you that he's well suited for this new kind of work. If you had a problem in your home life, you'd willingly pay money to spend an hour with him. God's guidance makes very good sense here.

As Charlie looks ahead, he still doesn't know for sure what his business card will say in another few years. He could wind up as a therapist…or a minister of pastoral care…or for that matter, as a business consultant for organizational and human development. We'll see.

In the meanwhile, he says his journaling is becoming more real, more honest, even blunt with every passing week. "I'm becoming more of a feeling person than I ever was before. My prayer life has more of a sense of emptying myself before God as well as more intercession, worship, and gratitude.

"Apparently, God can break up a life almost like a puzzle and put it back together in new ways I could never imagine."

In the midst of the dullest routine possible, God's creativity can break through.

- How would you describe Charlie Spicer's Second Wind in one sentence? Can you relate to an "ordinary life"? How would you describe one of your typical days to someone who had never met you?

  _____

  _____

  _____

  _____

  _____

  _____

  _____

- When you think of Moses' spending forty years tending sheep, what emotions and thoughts come to mind?

  _____

  _____

  _____

  Was God being fair or unfair?

  _____

  _____

  Was Moses doing what he was supposed to be doing?

  _____

  _____

  Is there anything about that forty-year stretch that makes you happy? angry? sad? afraid?

  _____

  _____

  _____

_____

_____

_____

- If you had been in Moses' sandals, would the story read the same? How would it differ?

_____

_____

_____

_____

_____

_____

- What do you think it will take in *your* life to experience a burning bush, blackboard, bookcase, band saw, or blender?

_____

_____

_____

_____

_____

_____

- How does the timeless nature of God affect the Second Wind? Can you think of two or three passages in the Old or New Testament that teach us that God is timeless? List them.

_____

_____

_____

_____

_____

_____

• What is the most important truth you gleaned from this chapter?

_____

_____

_____

• Based on what you read in this chapter, how can *you* get a Second Wind?

_____

_____

_____

_____

ON RISK

Howard R. Macy

The promise of the Second Wind involves many of the great themes of the gospel—hope, grace, forgiveness, and endurance, among others—all of which have been treated by great Christian minds through the centuries. In addition to our own contemporary viewpoint, we are including in this book a number of these classic voices.

In this excerpt, a professor at George Fox University in Oregon speaks about how spiritual growth is not always safe.

It is precisely the anticipation of risk that holds many of us back. We don't like risk, and even though the frontiers of spiritual growth require it, we prefer to avoid it. Not only would we like to have the frontiers of the spirit scouted out for us, we would also like to have the frontier fully tamed and settled, like a new suburban development with well-lighted streets and sewers installed, established zoning codes, houses built and finished save for seeding the lawn and planting the shrubs, shopping centers nearby, and adequate police protection. No pioneering for us—no danger from the dark wild, no felling trees or clearing boulders so that we can plant a subsistence garden, no climbing mountain passes or fording swollen streams. We prefer comfortable safety to risk.

The spiritual world, however, cannot be made suburban. It is always the frontier, and if we would live in it, we must accept and even rejoice that it remains untamed. The Ultimate Reality will not yield to our small-minded blueprints for the City of God.

Any realistic longing for God must wrestle with the apprehension that we don't know exactly what we're getting into. At times this life can be very uncomfortable, because we know that we will be changed without always knowing in what way. However, where there is discomfort, there is also security. As we pursue this life, a confidence grows that knowing God, whatever the risks, is safer and sweeter than any other path. We come to know deeply that ultimately this is not only the best but the only reasonable course.

Though we will not always live with our hearts in our throats, we should take up risk as a spiritual discipline. We need daily to yield our whole lives up to God, and we must examine them steadily to see whether we have declared any area off-limits to God's direction and transforming power. We must choose not just once but constantly to love God with all our hearts, souls, and strength, and to allow God completely to direct our living. We must choose perpetually to hold ourselves in this sometimes uncomfortable but secure place of risk.

The life of longing requires such vigilance, yet it is only by making the Lord our only joy that we can enter the life to which God still graciously calls us. "Our Lord finds our desires not too strong, but too weak," writes C. S. Lewis. "We are half-hearted creatures, fooling about with drink and sex and ambition when infinite joy is offered us.... We are far too easily pleased." Perpetual longing is the way of promise. "How happy those who...seek him with their whole heart" ([Psalm] 119:2).[1]

CHAPTER 3

DAMAGED GOODS

–Bill–

In the opening chapter of this book I regaled you with dazzling accounts of the ocean beach where I run…the sand, the surf, the lovely sunshine of your vacation dreams.

But I want you to know that our town is just like yours in many ways. We have yards and neighbors, we grow roses, and on Monday nights we put out the trash for collection. Recently our neighbors across the street decided to sell their place. Our real estate market is hot, so their home didn't last very long. In a matter of weeks the moving van arrived, and they packed up and were gone.

Except for a pile of trash.

Now I know it will be a blow to my suave image for you to hear the following, but it's true: I had the best time rooting through their stuff! In fact, they left on a Thursday, so I had a whole weekend to carefully analyze my neighbors' refuse before the Tuesday morning pickup.

You know the old saying "One man's trash is another man's treasure." Well, in with all the cans of old paint, boxes of wallpaper scraps, cracked shoes, and old clothes, I did find a leather briefcase right out of the 1920s. But the rest was pretty worn, tattered, and beat up. I didn't come home with much.

THE PRIEST AND HIS BOY

I know some human beings who, sadly, are like my neighbors' tattered items sitting by the curb. They once were shiny and new, full of promise and potential—until something very sad happened along the way. Somebody or something scratched their souls, marring their innocence. Their value on the marketplace of society took a dive from that time forward.

Such a man was John Hesler, who came to hear me speak awhile back and then told me his story. Growing up in a stable Catholic home in Schenectady, New York, in the 1950s, he was the oldest of five children. His dad, an engineer, and his stay-at-home mom took the family to mass every Sunday; in fact, "The church was our life," John says. "Two of my uncles were priests, an aunt was a nun, a cousin became a priest, and we all enjoyed a closeness in our family."

Coming up through twelve years of parochial school, John was active in Scouting and CYO (Catholic Youth Organization). He loved the church. He even got a part-time job there as a janitor during high school. When a new priest arrived in John's junior year who was outgoing and likable, John was naturally drawn to him. "He'd take me and my friends out for pizza and always seemed interested in what we were doing. He bought me a lot of gifts. He even gave me a set of keys to his car, which was tremendous, because none of us teenagers had cars back then.

"I loved the attention. He would heap loads of praise on me, and whenever he asked me to do something for him, I was eager to please him."

Sex was a very quiet topic in those days, something most parents couldn't bear to mention. The priest asked questions from time to time about what John and his friends were doing with girls…rather intimate questions, it seemed. But they didn't think much about it.

During John's senior year, the priest was transferred to a different parish not far away. John kept in touch, and when asked to come help out there, he readily agreed. One night the man invited him to stay overnight in the rectory.

"Again, I thought nothing of it. So after a day of work and then going out for something to eat, I went upstairs to sleep in the guest room. He came up after a while and began talking to me. At one point he sat on the edge of the bed where I was, and as he continued normal conversation on some ordinary topic…his hand began reaching under the covers.

"I absolutely froze. I couldn't believe what was happening. I was petrified. It took me a few minutes to finally get up the courage to say, 'Please don't.'"

The priest immediately stopped and began to apologize. "I'm so sorry—I should never have done that. Please forgive me." He went into a description of how lonely his life was as a priest and all the trials and problems he was facing. John immediately felt sorry for the man and began to accept the blame.

"Oh, that's okay," the boy said in a comforting tone. "I know you have a hard life." When the priest finally left the room, John lay staring at the ceiling. Somehow he knew this must be his fault.

BEWILDERED

One could wish that this was a one-time aberration, never to be repeated. But it was not. Over the next year, there were between twenty and thirty episodes where the priest would corner his young friend, begin to hug him, caress him, and then slip his hand inside the teenager's jeans. "I was terrified each time," John says. "I didn't know what to do. I felt like I couldn't talk to anybody. I mean, who would believe me? This man had a very strong personality, and there was no way an ordinary layperson, especially a young person like me, could go up against him."

The only defense John could muster was to avoid getting caught alone with the man. He would take friends along. His parents thought it odd that John wanted them to accompany him when he went to the rectory. Even their presence, however, did not solve the problem.

"John, let's go in the kitchen and fix a snack for your mom and dad," the priest would say in a cheerful voice.

"Sure, Father."

And within minutes, John would be pinned against the wall, with his unsuspecting parents right around the corner. Nothing salacious was ever verbalized; the man could be talking about the weather at the same time he was abusing John. His words and actions were totally disconnected.

The young man finally started to make excuses of not being available whenever the priest would call his home. Soon John headed off to the University of Connecticut. The episodes thus came to a stop, and the priest dropped out of his life. But the damage was done. John found himself terribly confused about sexuality and its proper place. It was revolting but also electrifying all at once.

"The only thing I kept telling myself at this point was that it had all been my fault. I must have done something to turn him on. I was bad; I was sinful; I was evil. Maybe I was homosexual. Whatever the case, I had caused an awful situation."

After two years of college, John fled to the opposite coast, feeling depressed and very lost. He landed a job at the Catholic Student Center next to the University of California, Berkeley, as director of religious services. There he tried to block out the past, plunging himself into leading worship and running other programs. He even wondered if he should become a priest himself.

But what was this mysterious force called sex, this passion that kept rising up within him? One day he saw an article in a Berkeley newspaper about local massage parlors. He decided to try one out.

"I was immediately hooked," he says. "It was so intriguing. When I had the attention of a woman in that dimly lit room, as phony as it was and even though I was paying for it, I felt like on some level I was being validated.

"Of course, as soon as I would walk outside again, I would feel horrible and guilty. I would vow never to do this again. My pledge would last about a month…and then I'd be right back again."

John's secret life of sexual addiction lasted a long time: twenty years. He ventured into pornography and the use of prostitutes. He knew his behavior was not only unhealthy but illegal and that he could be arrested at any time. Still he felt powerless to change. *I could never live without this,* he told himself.

Through the church he met a young woman he liked and began to date her. Neither of them knew what a normal relationship should be. They slept together from the very beginning. When they got married, "I seemed to check out emotionally," John admits. "I kept fantasizing and acting out. I basically didn't show up for the marriage." After four years his wife left him for another guy.

THE LONG ROAD BACK

Embarrassed but not yet ready to get help, John kept living his double life. He left the student center and got a job in the San Jose area as an environmental specialist, writing impact reports. Years went by. Sometime in his midthirties he sought therapy to understand what was going on in his life. However, he continued churning through one relationship after another, even getting engaged again at one point but then backing out.

"I was spending huge amounts of money," he recalls. "I kept 'upping the dosage,' if you will, having liaisons more frequently. I remember once being involved with a woman who had three kids and worrying about whether I might be giving her AIDS.

"About that time, I was listening to KCBS one Sunday night and heard an interview with Jed Diamond, whose popular book *Looking for Love in All the Wrong Places* had just come out. I was riveted; it was like he was telling my story. For the first time I realized there were other people in the world besides me whose idea of sexuality was all messed up.

"I called him and said, 'Thank you for that radio thing you did! I need help.' He referred me to a therapist down in San Jose, and soon I got into the Twelve Step program called Sex and Love Addicts Anonymous."

There he learned that help was available after all for the gashes in his psyche. He admitted, "There was a part of me that liked the attention. It felt good to be touched. But the context in which I was seeking this kind of touch was also so very wrong."

A therapist finally explained to John what he now calls the "missing piece"—that every sexual escapade of his was actually a form of re-molesting himself. Even though on a conscious level John would decry the things the priest had done to him so long ago, he was perpetuating the sensation. "I felt I had to give myself away sexually to get acceptance and love," he says. "Finally I got it through my head that 'I don't need to do this anymore. I can stop.'"

The Twelve Step people would talk about the Higher Power who was available to help, of course, but John was not at all interested at first. After all, hadn't it been a "man of God" who had plunged his life into such ruin? "I was convinced that God had not been there at all for me," he says. "I was disillusioned and disgusted. It didn't help that when I contacted the bishop of Albany to report this priest, I basically got a stock response and nothing further happened.

"But then I came to realize that my throwing God and Jesus on the scrap heap had only created a huge hole in my life. I came to see that God was not some abstract being intent on punishing me. Instead, he was a loving God who cared very deeply. He had not abandoned me at all. Every time I had called out and wanted help, he had provided people to call me, programs to assist me, and courage to keep going. I realized I had always been held, even cradled in his arms. I couldn't ignore the fact that he loved me very deeply."

In the early 1990s at a dance, John met a woman named Sandy, who was dealing with similar issues of sexual addiction. They became attracted to each other, although he recognized that "we were both terrified of true intimacy. We had to work from scratch, figuring out how to connect on a nonsexual basis. I didn't know what to do at first; I felt kind of lost."

In time they broke up, then resumed their friendship. There was an ugly scene when Sandy found out that John was also seeing a previous girlfriend on the side. She blew up at him, and it proved to be the wake-up call he needed. He stopped his acting out once and for all, pledging to rebuild trust with Sandy and her alone.

They married in 1997, and a son, Nicholas, was born the next year. "When we knew a child was on the way, we began looking for a church. As unusual as it may sound, we wound up back at a Catholic church—but this time with a very loving community led by a wonderful pastor. It was a whole different scene from my growing-up years. Our faith became much more personal and real."

A daughter, Emily, came along in 2001. John says today that one of his biggest joys in life is coming home from work and getting mobbed by his two young children. "I feel very grateful, very blessed," he says.

He still meets every Monday night with a men's support group he started in the early 1990s to help and encourage one another as they work through their masculinity issues. When asked for his favorite scriptures, he cites the promise of Jesus, "I am with you always, to the very end of the age" (Matthew 28:20). He also mentions the line of the Twenty-third

Psalm that says, "Even though I walk through the valley of the shadow of death, I will fear no evil, for you are with me" (verse 4). His long, two-decade valley has indeed now come to an end.

"My life today is not about being a victim," John adds. "Yes, certain things happened to me. But the best way to live my life is to go beyond all that, be positive, and face the future. I have a wife, two children, a good job, a supportive group of men—and my relationship with God. In other words, I'm well taken care of!"

RESTORED

To see a person such as John Hesler overcome his trauma is to view a miracle. It is evidence of the goodness of God, who has promised to settle accounts and stand by the abused. As he said through the prophet Jeremiah:

"All who devour you will be devoured;
     all your enemies will go into exile.
Those who plunder you will be plundered;
     all who make spoil of you I will despoil.
But I will restore you to health
     and heal your wounds,"
                              declares the LORD,
"because you are called an outcast,
     Zion for whom no one cares." (30:16-17)

He is, in fact, "the God of all grace, who called you to his eternal glory in Christ, after you have suffered a little while, will himself restore you and make you strong, firm and steadfast" (1 Peter 5:10).

None of this is meant to minimize the damage. There is no denying that some people in this world do dreadful things to each other, sending them into personal tailspins that seem to go on and on. The sufferers are not just making this up, and they often cannot "just get over it" on their own. It may take both outside assistance and the fresh breath of God's Spirit to push away the smoke and darkness, bringing new vitality and wholeness.

The beauty of the gospel—some would say its outrageous claim—is that damaged men and women can be restored. Adults can actually change! They are not locked in their destructive patterns; they can be different in the future than they've been in the past. Is that too much to hope for? Only if we tell ourselves it is.

Psalm 71 says:

Though you have made me see troubles, many and bitter,
    you will restore my life again;
from the depths of the earth
    you will again bring me up.
You will increase my honor
    and comfort me once again. (verses 20-21)

For the traumatized, there is indeed a Second Wind.

Personal Journal

- Can you imagine the pain and trauma John Hesler experienced? If so, why? What sort of trauma in your life might cause you to identify with him? If, on the other hand, you can't relate to John, jot down your thoughts about this phrase: Have you ever felt like damaged goods?

  _____

  _____

  _____

  _____

  _____

- Work on the chart below by reflecting on the terms that describe suffering in our lives from Jeremiah 30 and Psalm 71. Then look at the words of hope and healing.

Words of Scripture	_What They Mean_	_What They Mean to Me_
All who devour you		
All your enemies		
Those who plunder you		
All who make spoil of you		
Your health		
Your wounds		
An outcast		
See troubles many and bitter		
From the depths of the earth		
Will be devoured		
Will go into exile		
Will be plundered		

Words of Scripture	What They Mean	What They Mean to Me
I will despoil		
I will restore		
Heal your wounds		
Zion		
Restore my life again		
You will bring me up		

- How do those words of healing translate into a Second Wind in your life? Choose one or two of those phrases most relevant to your situation in order to answer.

  _____

  _____

  _____

  _____

- In this chapter we find these words: "The beauty of the gospel—some would say its outrageous claim—is that damaged men and women can be restored. Adults can actually change! They are not locked in their destructive patterns; they can be different in the future than they've been in the past. Is this too much to hope for? Only if we tell ourselves it is." What does that mean to you in your current situation?

  _____

  _____

  _____

  _____

  _____

  _____

- Spend a few minutes in prayer, asking God to help you understand his message for you from this chapter.

- What is the most important truth you gleaned from this chapter?

  _____

  _____

  _____

  _____

- Based on what you read in this chapter, how can *you* get a Second Wind?

  _____

  _____

  _____

  _____

  _____

On Forgiveness

Matthew Henry (1662–1714)

A warm-hearted English minister some four hundred years ago, Matthew Henry often began working before five o'clock in the morning on his commentary—a project that consumed the last ten years of his life. Even then he finished only through the book of Acts; his ministerial friends completed the rest from his notes and writings.

In this section on Matthew 18:21-35, he explains how Jesus stretched Peter's understanding of forgiveness.

Peter's question concerning this matter (v. 21); *Lord, how oft shall my brother trespass against me, and I forgive him?* Will it suffice to do it *seven times?* He takes it for granted that he must forgive; Christ had before taught his disciples this lesson (ch. 6:14), and Peter has not forgotten it. He knows that he must not only not bear a grudge against his brother, or meditate revenge, but be as good a friend as ever, and forget the injury.

He thinks it is a great matter to forgive till seven times…supposing that if a man had any way abused him seven times, though he were ever so desirous to be reconciled, he might then abandon his society, and have no more to do with him.…

There is a proneness in our corrupt nature to stint ourselves in that which is good, and to be afraid of doing too much in religion, particularly of forgiving too much, though we have so much forgiven us.

Christ's direct answer to Peter's question; *I say not unto thee, Until seven times* (he never intended to set up any such bounds), but, *Until seventy times seven;* a certain number for an indefinite one, but a great one. It does not look well for us to keep count of the offences done against us by our brethren. There is something of ill-nature in scoring up the injuries we forgive, as if we would allow ourselves to be revenged when the measure is full. God keeps an account (Deu. 32:34), because he is the Judge, and vengeance is his; but we must not, lest we be found stepping into his throne. It is necessary to the preservation of peace, both within and without, to pass by injuries, without reckoning how often; to forgive, and forget. God multiplies his pardons, and so should we, Ps. 78:38. It intimates that we should make it our constant practice to forgive injuries, and should accustom ourselves to it till it becomes habitual.

Regarding the parable of the demanding servant:

The parable is a comment upon the fifth petition of the Lord's prayer, *Forgive us our trespasses, as we forgive them that trespass against us.* Those, and those only, may expect to be forgiven of God, who forgive their brethren....

Sinners are commonly careless about the pardon of their sins, till they come under the arrests of some awakening word, some startling providence, or approaching death, and then, *Wherewith shall I come before the Lord?* Mic. 6:6. How easily, how quickly, can God bring the proudest sinner to his feet; Ahab to his sackcloth, Manasseh to his prayers, Pharaoh to his confessions, Judas to his restitution, Simon Magus to his supplication, Belshazzar and Felix to their tremblings. The stoutest heart will fail, when God sets the sins in order before it....

God looked with pity on mankind in general, because miserable, and sent his Son to be a Surety for them; he looks with pity on particular penitents, because sensible of their misery (their hearts broken and contrite), and accepts them in the Beloved. There is forgiveness with God for the greatest sins, if they be repented of. Though the debt was vastly great, he *forgave it all,* Matt. 18:32. Though our sins be very numerous and very heinous, yet, upon gospel terms, they may be pardoned....

We must *from our hearts* forgive. We do not forgive our offending brother aright, nor acceptably, if we do not forgive from the heart; for that is it that God looks at. No malice must be harboured there, nor ill will to any person, one or another; no projects of revenge must be hatched there, nor desires of it, as there are in many who outwardly appear peaceable and reconciled. Yet this is not enough; we must from the heart desire and seek the welfare even of those that have offended us....

Those that do not *forgive their brother's trespasses,* did never truly repent of their own, nor ever truly believe the gospel; and therefore that which is *taken away* is only what *they seemed to have,* Lu. 8:18. This is intended to teach us, that *they shall have judgment without mercy, that have showed no mercy,* Jam. 2:13. It is indispensably necessary to pardon and peace, that we not only *do justly,* but *love mercy.* It is an essential part of that religion which is *pure and undefiled before God and the Father,* of that *wisdom from above,* which *is gentle, and easy to be entreated.*[1]

CHAPTER 4

WHO'S IN CONTROL?

—Dean—

Suppose you were taking a class in psychology or ethics, and the instructor came in one day with the following activity:

"Take out a piece of paper and draw a line down the middle. Mark the left column 'Good' and the right column 'Bad.'

"I will give you a series of simple words. Write down each of them in one column or the other."

He then begins the list: cholera, embezzlement, kindness, sunshine.

You wouldn't have much trouble sorting these out. The first two obviously go on the right, the second two on the left.

But then things get a little more complex. He pronounces the word "control."

Well, we certainly don't want to live in a society that's out of *control*. We much prefer a life of order and predictability. Most of us work in companies that have a financial *controller*—the person who watches the balance of income and expense in order to make sure that, among other things, our paychecks don't bounce. We like that.

On the other hand, control in the hands of an Adolf Hitler or a Saddam Hussein can be a nightmare. We've all dealt with people of ill intent as well as those who meant well but were just *overcontrolling* as they tried to boss our lives beyond reason.

Generally speaking, we like to control our own destinies. We prefer to be in charge of ourselves, thank you very much. Autonomy is a cherished value. Even if we mess ourselves up…even if we make mistakes…well, at least they were *our* mistakes.

WE KNOW BEST (WE THINK)

Sometimes the dead spot in our lives, the reason we're "stuck," the cause of our faded dreams and sagging energy is that we have tried to control our lives to an unhealthy degree. We didn't mean to, of course. But we have so tightly gripped our events and decisions that we have put ourselves off the smooth road and into the gravel. We haven't listened to the voice of God quietly telling us to turn the steering wheel differently.

To cite a poignant real-life example, let me tell you the story of a woman named Sandy Bolte.

If you had stopped by her suburban Denver home in the 1980s, you would have met a well-organized mother of three with a welcoming smile. Thanks to the steady salary of her husband, Dennis, a government attorney, she got to stay home and do what she loved: raise kids, volunteer at their school, teach Sunday school at the Presbyterian church, go to women's Bible studies. Little Denise, Dennis Jr. (called DJ), and Christopher completed the picture of the ideal family.

What Sandy would not have told you was that she was a closet junkie. Her long-running obsession with tranquilizers and muscle relaxants had started back in her late twenties. At first, the drugs were legitimately needed: At age twenty-one she had broken her back and had surgery to fuse the vertebrae. Then as a newlywed a few years later the first two children had come along less than a year apart. "I was hit with terrific back spasms and pain," she recalls. "The narcotics helped me get on top of all that. Over the years the back problem gradually went away, but the pills continued.

"What I didn't know, however, was what the Librium and the Fiorinal with codeine were doing to me. This second combination, by the way, is so strong it has since been taken off the market. My feelings were numbed; I didn't know my true emotions for all that time. I hadn't cried in who knows how long."

Sandy was into her early forties, with two children growing into teenagers, when something happened to unsettle her control. She developed a bleeding ulcer. Her doctor analyzed the various factors and came to the belated realization that this calm-looking homemaker and mother was in fact addicted to the medication she had been taking for sixteen years. He ordered her into a thirty-day residential treatment program to wean her off the drugs.

"Nobody told me it would be years before I'd be any sort of normal again," Sandy says. "I began seeing a psychiatrist. All of a sudden I was very, very, *very* depressed, even suicidal. It was awful. The bottom dropped out of my life."

Sandy knew one way to relieve her malaise, however. She had been an x-ray technician before she got married, so she knew how to work the medical system. The soothing medicine she craved was still waiting at any corner pharmacy. Thus came the first day she picked up the phone and called Walgreen's.

"Hello?"

"Yes, this is Karen in Dr. Joel Martin's office," Sandy lied. "I have another patient prescription for you, please. This one's for 'Betty Schuman,' S-C-H-U-M-A-N; give her a thirty count of Librium ten milligrams, dosage twice a day with food."

"Got it," came the reply from the pharmacist's young helper. "We'll take care of it."

And a couple of hours later, Sandy would drive down to Walgreen's, edge up to the counter, and calmly ask for the Schuman prescription. The pharmacist, as she predicted, had been much too harried to verify the validity of her order. With a quick forged signature and an exchange of cash, she would be on her way with yet another vial of powerful narcotics to keep her nerves subdued and her composure in place. This was easy.

"In an odd sort of way," Sandy admits, "pushing the phony 'scripts' was almost as addictive as the drugs themselves. It was a challenge to pull off, an exciting adventure to see if I could get away with it yet another time."

With no limits on access, her intake began to climb. Before long, she was gulping down fifteen to twenty pills at a time, four to five times a day. Her spree lasted ten months, until a diligent pharmacist finally happened to check back with the doctor to confirm what Sandy had requested. The charade suddenly came apart as police knocked on the front door of the Bolte home.

Sandy found herself in court, embarrassed, ashamed, repentant. She told the judge she had made a big mistake and pleaded for leniency. He handed down a deferred sentence of one year, provided Sandy would go back into drug rehabilitation treatment. She eagerly agreed.

"I had a perfect chance to straighten up," she says. "If I would stay out of trouble for a year, my record would be wiped clean.

"But that didn't happen."

SPIRALING DOWN

Not long after finishing the drug program, Sandy returned home—and returned to her narcotics. At this point her husband was losing patience. "In years past I'd always been the steady one in the marriage," she says, "making most of the day-to-day decisions at home so he could just work. Now I couldn't do that anymore, and he let me know I'd better shape up or ship out.

"I went into psychotherapy again. I urged him to come along with me, but after a couple of joint appointments, he said he didn't want to do that anymore.

"I was in no state to function. I kept downing huge doses of pills and was in and out of treatment programs for the next year. Meanwhile, our home was just totally unraveling."

Sandy was not only losing control, she was losing hope. Her extended family was unable to help. The church seemed not to know what to do with her. Communication with Dennis had shut down. She still remembers their last conversation, when she asked in dismay, "What are we going to do—just let the attorneys sort it out?"

His reply: "Yeah."

Soon thereafter, Sandy left home for good. She set up her own apartment. As the silence and the loneliness bore down on her, she found solace, of course, only in more drugs. And again, she got caught.

This time the sentence was more severe. She was placed in Community Corrections for eight months—a program in which the offenders must live in an old motel under surveillance, keeping a curfew, but have permission to hold down a daytime job. "It's your last chance before prison," Sandy says. "I functioned really well there for a while. My job, in fact, was working in a Christian bookstore!

"But when they let me return to my own home, I started using tranquilizers and painkillers again. I had no purpose in life. Somehow in all this upheaval, I had lost myself. I had little or no self-esteem. I didn't know who I was. The Lord I thought I knew, I didn't know intimately. I hadn't surrendered all that I was to him.

"I flunked out one more time, and that was it for the judge: He sentenced me to eighteen months at CWCF—the Colorado Women's Correctional Facility in Cañon City."

The former suburbanite cried for five straight days in the county's interim processing center, shaking with panic at what lay ahead for her. She was about to be locked up with fist-swinging brawlers and aggressive lesbians; she knew she was doomed. "You'll never survive," more than one person told her. "They'll kill you before you know what hit you."

There was no postponing the inevitable, however. The day came that Sandy was driven 120 miles southwest from the Denver area to the small, mountain-ringed town of Cañon City. The beauty of the snow-capped Rockies stood in silent contrast to the gray ugliness of her institutional future. She knew she had blown half a dozen opportunities to straighten up and avoid this fate.

"It's a whole revelation to walk through those gates and hear them clang shut behind you. You've lost everything. You can do absolutely nothing without asking permission—even go to the bathroom.

"You have to get up at 5:45 in order to eat breakfast at 6:00 and then be at your job at 7:00. Mine was ground maintenance. You get off work at 3:30 in the afternoon. That means lots of time to do nothing but put up with loud rap music.

"The homosexuality was quite obvious, although there were many of us who were not gay. One of my cells was right next to a lesbian couple, which was an awful situation. Another time I had a lesbian cellmate.

"Somehow, though, the Lord protected me. Nothing ever happened to me. They knew I claimed to be a Christian, and that's not a popular thing in prison. You get a lot of ridicule. But they never threatened me physically. Of course, I was fifty years old and white, while most of the others were in their twenties and were minorities. So I wasn't of any particular value to them in their peer groups." As for fights between inmates, Sandy saw only one during her time in prison.

A local woman named Jan came to lead a Bible study every Sunday night for about ten inmates. "I'd never look people in the eye," Sandy says, "and she'd come over, pull up my chin, and say, 'I love you, and the Lord loves you. You're a worthwhile person.' She did this over and over.

"Finally it began to click. *Maybe she's right. Maybe I didn't commit the unpardonable sin. Maybe God still loves me.*"

On Mother's Day, Jan said to the group, "Let's have a time of prayer now for all our kids."

"I don't pray for my kids," Sandy fired back. She had totally turned off the notion of family; she had no idea what Denise, DJ, and Christopher were even doing these days. As for her ex-husband, she knew he had quickly remarried.

More than that, Sandy assumed God couldn't care less about any kind of prayer from her, even for innocent children.

Jan jumped to respond to Sandy's brush-off. "Oh, you must!" she cried. "Even in prison, you have to ask God to watch over your kids." Soon the circle of women began lifting up names of children in sincere intercession.

When six months had passed, Sandy was eligible for parole. Because she had behaved herself, the officials told her she would be released to go back to Denver.

Sandy wasn't so sure she *wanted* out. "I'm not gonna make this," she told the parole office.

"But they didn't believe me. Although I had come closer to the Lord, I knew something still wasn't right; I wasn't strong enough to stay clean. So I went back to Denver—and within two months I'd violated the parole and was back in the Denver County Jail."

Sandy's parole officer came to see her and viewed the situation as a minor lapse. "Well, now, we'll get you out of here, and you can resume your parole," he said.

Sandy's face grew serious. "No, you don't understand," she replied. "Send me back to prison. That's my only salvation."

So back to Cañon City she went to finish out her full sentence. This time the spiritual awakening that had started before took full root. During the next nine months or so, "I really did totally surrender control of my life to the Lord—every morning. It was a turning point at last. On the job outside doing groundskeeping work, I spent a lot of time down on my knees—praying and crying to the Lord, *If I ever get out of here again, something has to change within me.*"

Jan would write original Bible studies just for Sandy. She would also send her mail during the week—the only mail Sandy ever received. In time Sandy got a new cellmate who was warm and supportive, who insisted that both of them go regularly to Sunday chapel meetings and also do their Bible studies.

"It was during these days that I began to claim Jeremiah 29:11, that wonderful scripture that says, ' "For I know the plans I have for you," declares the LORD, "plans to prosper you and not to harm you, plans to give you hope and a future." ' I would literally say those words every morning."

BACK ON TRACK

Sandy Bolte has been out of prison since August 1993. She still lives in Cañon City, working now as a counselor in a rehab center, guiding others like herself to conquer the tormenting issues of drug abuse. She is extremely cautious about what medicine she takes, even for a headache. "My doctor knows all about my past, so he won't even give me cough medicine with codeine. Anything I swallow has to be nonnarcotic unless I'm in a hospital where they can monitor me."

Along with the physical traces of the past, there are emotional scars as well. Sandy's daughter is still too wounded to speak to her mother. Sandy's older son, DJ, has managed to cross the gulf, however. He showed up at the funeral of Sandy's mother, giving Sandy her first glimpse of him in more than a decade. No longer a squeaky-voiced adolescent, he had turned into a handsome young man. Today he's an architectural engineer in northern Colorado.

When her youngest, Christopher, graduated from high school, Sandy was there—the only one of her three whom she got to see in a cap and gown. He even moved in with her during college, and the two of them grew quite close. Eventually he finished a bachelor's degree in psychology.

Sandy knows her life is stabilized once again because of God's steady hand. "I just feel the Lord's presence so much when I pray or read the Scriptures," she says. "God has restored me more than I ever dreamed could be possible."

COMMANDER IN CHIEF

When we surrender control of our lives to God, it frees him to let the Second Wind blow. This is not a denial of our talents or abilities; in fact, God uses them more impressively to accomplish more things and greater wholeness than we ever could on our own. He is not squelching us; he is unleashing us to a brighter future.

When Joshua was about to lead the Israelites into battle against Jericho, he certainly had his own plans. He'd been looking forward to this opportunity for forty years in the desert. Finally he would get to march on the Promised Land.

And then something very strange happened.

Near Jericho, he looked up and saw a man standing in front of him with a drawn sword in his hand. Joshua went up to him and asked, "Are you for us or for our enemies?"

"Neither," he replied, "but as commander of the army of the
LORD I have now come." Then Joshua fell facedown to the ground
in reverence. (Joshua 5:13-14)

This was definitely a "who's in charge?" moment. Joshua thought he
was the four-star general, and all the colonels and captains and enlisted
troops would obey his orders. Then the unusual man with the drawn sword
showed up to say, "Excuse me, but I'll take over now. Just follow my lead."

In the next chapter we find out what strange strategy the man had in
mind. March around the city blowing trumpets? Crazy! This made no
sense to any graduate of a military academy.

But Joshua, having surrendered control to the angel of the Lord, did as
instructed and as a result won a massive victory at Jericho. Nobody would
have predicted this odd turn of events. Nobody but God.

If we would salute the Lord as the true commander of our lives, admit-
ting that we are his subordinates, we might be surprised at the marvelous
outcomes.

It's interesting to notice that Joshua later had trouble remembering the
lesson of the man with the sword. Chapter 9 of his book tells about the day
a group showed up in camp claiming to be from far away. They had heard
about Israel's impressive blitz and wanted to sign a peace treaty.

The only trouble was, they *weren't* from far away. They were from the
next city over the hill and had only been to the costume shop for worn-out
clothes and travel equipment. Their disguise was convincing.

In this moment, Joshua made a critical error: He forgot to check with
his commander.

The men of Israel sampled their provisions *but did not inquire of the
LORD*. Then Joshua made a treaty of peace with them to let them
live, and the leaders of the assembly ratified it by oath.

Three days after they made the treaty with the Gibeonites, the Israelites heard that they were neighbors, living near them. (Joshua 9:14-16, emphasis added)

This led to a messy situation. "The whole assembly grumbled against the leaders," says verse 18. What a bonehead mistake, and now they had to figure out what to do with these Gibeonites, who had been promised peace and safety right in the middle of the land that was supposed to become Israel's.

By the next chapter, when five kings decided to march against Gibeon, the case got even stickier. The Gibeonites came running and crying, "You have to help us! You have to protect us! You promised!" One can just imagine Joshua with his forehead in his hands, grimacing at the jam he'd gotten into. He had no choice but to haul out his entire army and rise to the defense of these tricksters. You can imagine how popular that was with the Israelite rank and file.

God's best comes to the person who realizes who is meant to be in control—and never forgets it. God knows the difference between smart and dumb, wise and foolish, safe and dangerous. His plan is, as Jeremiah said, "to prosper you and not to harm you,...to give you hope and a future." The obvious move on our part is to stand aside and let him lead.

- How did you feel when you read Sandy Bolte's story? Is there anything about her story that reminded you of your life? Jot down your thoughts.

  _____

  _____

  _____

  _____

- How would you define the word *control?* How important is control to you in the current circumstances of your life? If you could change one thing about "control over your life," what would that one change be?

  _____

  _____

  _____

  _____

  _____

  _____

- Can you identify with Joshua's desire to control? Lately, are your days more like Joshua 5, where God is given control of the situation, or are they like Joshua 9, where we go on about our lives and don't "inquire of the Lord"? What are three or four things you can do to give God control more consistently?

  _____

  _____

  _____

_____

_____

_____

_____

- Take a few minutes for prayer. Ask God for help in yielding control to him on a more regular basis.

- Jeremiah 29:11 is a verse Sandy Bolte would claim as her own at the beginning of each day. Take some time to commit that verse to memory. Write it out on a three-by-five card, and begin saying it aloud over and over again. Before long, it will be yours!

- What is the most important truth you gleaned from this chapter?

_____

_____

_____

_____

- Based on what you read in this chapter, how can *you* get a Second Wind?

_____

_____

_____

_____

_____

ON THE NECESSITY OF COMING CLEAN

Patrick Kavanaugh

In his day Franz Liszt was famed as the world's finest pianist—number one in his class.

Well behind him in reputation, many lesser pianists attempted to scratch out careers, sometimes stooping to unscrupulous methods to capture attention. One young woman in this group (her name has mercifully been forgotten) concocted a notorious whopper to attract a larger audience. For a recital in Berlin, she advertised extensively that she was a "pupil of Liszt" (whom she had never even met!).

She assumed she could get away with this. Who would know her secret? And surely Liszt would never find out.

Imagine her horror when, on the very morning of her publicized performance, the newspapers announced that Liszt himself had just arrived in Berlin. What could she do now? Her duplicity would be publicly exposed, and she would be disgraced. After wrestling with remorse, she decided to go to Liszt and confess her misdeed.

Begging for an interview at his hotel, the woman entered his suite in trepidation, fearing the master's wrath for such a disrespectful offence. With many tears she confessed—and waited, expecting to be banished from his presence.

Far from showing fury, the great Liszt attended her thoughtfully as he worked through an idea in his head.

The woman listened incredulously as Liszt quietly asked her the name of each piece on her program. Selecting one, he asked her to sit at his piano and play it for him.

She began. Liszt listened and eventually interrupted with several hints about how to perform the composition. Then he smiled, and with a pat on the cheek, he dismissed her: "Now, my dear, you may call yourself a pupil of Liszt."

By his actions he went beyond forgiveness. He helped her save face.

That wiser and humbler woman left the hotel, graced with a Christlike gesture of clemency.[1]

ELIGIBLE FOR GOOD THINGS

—Dean—

Like a coin with two sides, however, the message of the previous chapter on letting God control our lives must be matched with the need for us to make right choices even when we'd rather not. At whatever points along the way we face the option of one road versus another, we must select the one that God is willing to bless rather than the opposite.

Psalm 15:1 poses the question, "LORD, who may dwell in your sanctuary? Who may live on your holy hill?" In other words, who's in line for God's favor? What does it take to qualify?

The rest of the psalm is a list of answers. Near the end of verse 4 comes this attention-getting item: "[He] who keeps his oath even when it hurts." When we promise to do something—and later on, that "something" turns out to be terribly inconvenient or uncomfortable—God expects us to take a deep breath and keep our word regardless. He's not impressed with those who fudge and reinterpret and adjust their pledge.

In performing a marriage ceremony, I sometimes read this psalm aloud. Looking out at the gathering of family and friends in the pews, I know they are sitting there listening to the couple's lofty rhetoric of wedding vows and thinking to themselves, *I hope they really mean all that!* So do I. That's why I emphasize this somewhat blunt scripture. It makes the point that, five or ten years later, whether or not you feel like continuing to "love, honor, and cherish" your mate, "forsaking all others and cleaving wholly unto" him or her "as long as you both shall live," God wants you to carry through. That is the kind of scenario he can enrich and prosper.

Many other examples could be cited: the promise to pray consistently about a given need, to pick up a certain responsibility at our church, or to give God his portion of our paycheck, among others. We have all told God we'd do certain things but then struggled to follow up.

This only creates barriers for the Second Wind, like a range of mountains that blocks the cleansing breezes and traps the smog in a valley.

THE RELUCTANT MESSENGER

The Bible tells about a man who learned this principle. He was a prophet of God named Jonah. His job, of course, was to speak God's messages to the people.

He did fine, the book of 2 Kings tells us, when the prophecy was upbeat. He predicted that a certain king would expand the boundaries of Israel, and it came true just as Jonah had said (see 2 Kings 14:25).

But when the Lord assigned him to travel northeast and preach judgment to Nineveh, capital city of Israel's great enemy, Jonah freaked out. Why? He could just imagine that he might be successful…the pagan people might repent and turn to Jehovah…and then what would happen to Israel's privileged position as the spiritual hub of the world? Jonah was a loyal Israelite, and he didn't want to see a Nineveh revival at all. He promptly headed west.

As everyone knows, there was no peace or rest for this prophet on the run. It got so bad that even the ship captain, who didn't know God, was pleading with Jonah to talk to God. "How can you sleep?" the man cried (Jonah 1:6). "Get up and call on your god! Maybe he will take notice of us, and we will not perish."

What does it require for the almighty God to "take notice of us"? That's what we all crave, of course, whether in a typhoon on the open sea or in any other kind of distress. We want God to save our necks, to bless us, to rescue us from trouble.

But he doesn't do so for the disobedient. He keeps ratcheting up the pressure, in fact. Not until Jonah wound up inside the great fish and began to pray did God hear him say the crucial words:

I, with a song of thanksgiving,
    will sacrifice to you.
What I have vowed I will make good.
    Salvation comes from the LORD. (Jonah 2:9)

At last Jonah was ready and willing to do what his calling required. Within minutes the fish had ejected the prophet, and he was on his way to Nineveh. There his words brought an entire metropolis to its knees.

Who would have expected that Jonah would end up being the one smashing success among the Old Testament prophets? Taken as a group, they mostly failed. Jeremiah was consistently mocked or else ignored; Amos was thrown out of the king's court; Ezekiel was told in the very beginning that nobody would listen to him. Even Isaiah and Daniel managed only tentative responses from the monarchs they addressed.

But "the Ninevites believed God. They declared a fast, and all of them, from the greatest to the least, put on sackcloth" (3:5). The lives of perhaps a half-million people were spared as a result.

Why did the pagan Assyrians listen and respond so wholeheartedly to this man? It is tantalizing to wonder whether Jonah told them about his voyage. Some Bible students have suggested that even his skin and hair might have been bleached by the acids of the fish's stomach, lending credence to his story. After all, Jesus did comment that "Jonah was a sign to the Ninevites" (Luke 11:30).

But whether Jonah related his past on the streets of Nineveh or not, the results of his ministry force us to recognize that once you do what God wants you to do, amazing results come. The same is true for us today.

The sooner we get over arguing with God and with ourselves about the correct course of action, the sooner he can bless our efforts. The renaissance we crave lies on the far side of obedience.

A LONG AND WINDING ROAD

Nelson and Judy Padgett learned this the hard way, by marrying, divorcing, and then marrying each other again. When you meet this gracious couple, now nearing retirement age, you have no idea the torturous trail they took to get to their present stability.

Both of them were raised with plenty of church input—he Pentecostal, she Catholic—but failed to grasp what a Christian marriage was intended to be. "I knew the church was against divorce," says Judy, "but they never really said why. Or at least I didn't hear them. Divorce was just one of the long list of sins you had to confess. So I pretty much bypassed that part."

Nelson's mother took him to church regularly, although his dad stayed home. The only flicker of awakening came at age seventeen, when Nelson had joined the army and came home on leave after basic training. "There was a revival meeting under way," he explains in his soft Kentucky accent, "and I went to the altar one night. It was a genuine encounter with God. My life changed as a result, but not to the extent it should have, especially when I got back to my base and then soon shipped out for the Korean War."

Like the seed in Jesus' parable that fell on rocky soil, all evidence of spiritual life soon withered away. Following Nelson's combat tour in Korea, he came back, spent a year in the civilian world, then reenlisted, in the air force this time. He spent most of a full twenty-year career as a jet engine mechanic. "I was a total heathen," he says with a chuckle. "The only time I went to church was for a wedding or a funeral." His first marriage produced four children but ended tragically with his wife's death in a car accident. Subsequently, he married again.

Judy, meanwhile, was busy raising five children of her own. When the youngest became old enough for her to return to the workplace, she found a job at a home improvement company, surrounded by men who paid her the attention she wasn't getting from her husband. One of her fellow employees was Nelson.

"Our story is not something to be proud of," they both say today. "We started dating, even though we both were still technically married." After both had divorced their mates, they decided to marry each other. "We had no idea what we were doing."

The outdoor wedding took place in Louisville on September 7, 1985, officiated by a Unitarian minister whom Nelson's sister had lined up. Judy now admits that she headed into the marriage assuming she could get her new husband to convert to Catholicism. But Nelson wasn't that pliable. The two also disagreed from time to time on parenting issues with Judy's daughter Becky, a senior in high school who lived with them, the one remaining child for whom they were responsible.

By the summer of 1987 "we concluded, 'Well, this is not working—

we'll just go our separate ways,'" Nelson relates. "We weren't mad at each other. We weren't having money fights or screaming at each other. We just didn't know what the commitment of marriage was all about."

Judy adds, "It's easy to talk yourself into another divorce if you've already done it once. Neither one of us was going to change, and both of us were equally willing to split. So we filled out the paperwork, went down to the courthouse, got the matter finalized—and went out to lunch!"

The lack of rancor made it possible for contact to continue. They stayed in the same city and kept in touch, usually through weekly phone calls. More than a year passed. A small twinge of regret began to creep into both their hearts.

"One night we were talking," Nelson remembers, "and one of us said, 'You know, we could get married again and maybe make this work, if we could find a church…'"

Judy explains, "That was our way of saying we needed the Lord. But we couldn't come out and state it that directly. We just talked about finding a church that both of us could accept. God was starting to open our hearts."

Just then evangelist James Robison came to town for a crusade. Nelson went—and like the night at the revival meeting back when he was a teenager, he responded once again to the invitation. He calls it a rededication of his life to Christ.

At the same general time, Judy went to see her priest at the Catholic church she had always attended. "I need help," she told the cleric. "Look at me: I was divorced once; then I got married, then divorced again. Not very good for a Catholic, right? What's going on?"

The priest quietly replied, "It sounds to me like you need a relationship with Jesus." He proceeded to give her some practical instruction, and from that point on, Judy began something of a running conversation with

God. In retrospect, she would not say she was born again, but she was at least headed in the right direction.

"The Lord seemed to put it into both our hearts that we'd made a mistake by divorcing...that with just a little effort, we could make this work," says Nelson. "But we knew, and openly said to each other, that we could not do this again without the Lord."

Together Again

The couple began church shopping. The first two congregations they visited proved to be too high-energy for Judy, who was accustomed to the quiet dignity of the Mass. On the third try, they found a Christian church that was just right for them both. The pastor was preaching through the book of Nehemiah. "It was all about rebuilding the broken-down walls in your life," Judy says with amazement. "How appropriate for us!"

Soon they made an appointment with this pastor, who came to meet them at Nelson's place. He proved to be a wonderful guide. They told him they were thinking about maybe getting married again but that they needed help to succeed this time.

Soon both Nelson and Judy had made a firm commitment to follow Jesus. They began a series of premarital counseling sessions with the pastor. He told them, "When you come to the wedding, there will be three of you at the altar. You don't just remarry each other; you also pledge yourselves to God. From that point on, you're one with God as well as with each other."

The small wedding on January 21, 1989, was attended only by the couple's various children and grandchildren plus Judy's brother. Their parents on both sides were understandably hesitant about this second round. The kids, however, were happy to see them back together. Judy wore the same off-white evening dress she had worn at her first wedding to Nelson three and a half years before.

On the second Sunday after the wedding, the newlyweds were baptized at the church. The pastor baptized Nelson and then allowed Nelson to baptize Judy. It proved to be a dramatic moment. "When I came up out of that water," she says, "I just knew I was truly born again. I thought I was going to explode! The power of the Holy Spirit was so overwhelming.

"And it didn't go away. I called the pastor from work the next day to say, 'What is going on?! I feel like I'm about to burst. I'm flushed; I could just scream.'"

"Oh, it's okay," he responded. "Don't worry—it'll go away!"

Actually, that wasn't what Judy wanted. She was more hungry than ever to experience the fullness of God's blessing in her life.

She found herself being profoundly moved by the music she was hearing at church and on Christian radio—both the new praise styles as well as the historic hymns. In time she and Nelson relocated to a large and growing charismatic fellowship on the edge of the city. Once again, the very first sermon made a powerful impact, this time on Nelson.

"Pastor Ted spoke about the commitment of marriage—I can remember it to this day. He talked about making a covenant with God and how you definitely do not want to mess around with that. I'd never thought about these kinds of things. It was radical for me."

Today, more than a decade later, Nelson and Judy are still in this church, serving as part of the elders group. They also coordinate Communion for the congregation, which has now grown to some nine thousand. Nelson is an usher, and they counsel young couples in need of spiritual guidance. "We don't broadcast our personal story a lot, but we do let them know that it's possible to get along, to stay married—that it is God's will to do so," says Nelson.

"Our hearts have just totally changed. Before they were hard; we didn't understand commitment. We didn't understand servanthood either. We've just grown so much."

They admit that their life together has not always been easy. "But the word *divorce* never comes into our vocabulary," says Judy. "Neither of us would ever walk away. Instead, we'll stay right here and work through things. That is so much easier when you've got the Lord in your life. We tell Satan to get out of the way and leave us alone.

"The truth is, our first marriage could have worked just as well as it has the last fourteen years had we known the Lord. Now our life is fun. I feel safe. Several of our grown children have come to know the Lord as well.

"God can bless a couple when they finally yield to him."

Beyond the Pain

Isn't it intriguing to think about God looking down from heaven at all of our lives and seeing the potential for joy, for balance, for healthy relationships—if only we would give him cooperation? Jesus said that while "the thief" (meaning Satan) is interested in stealing, killing, and destroying, Jesus' whole purpose is quite the opposite: "that they may have life, and have it to the full" (John 10:10).

So many people wrongly assume that God wants to constrict us, to dominate us, to keep us from enjoying ourselves. They think he's in the business of pulling the fences tighter and higher around our lives, shutting out all sense of splash and delight.

Quite the opposite is true. He *wants* us to smile. He *wants* us to succeed. He *wants* our marriages to be healthy and long-lasting. He is also experienced enough to know that we humans need help in making that happen. We're wisdom-deficient on our own. We're "relationally challenged." But as we accept his input and even surrender to his greater knowledge, he can bring us into a wonderful season of fulfillment and usefulness.

In whatever situation you find yourself, keep asking the Lord what part you should play. In his grand scheme, he sees the big picture far more clearly than you ever will. Your role is to fall in line with his strategy, to do the right thing now even though you've strayed in the past, and then to watch what God will do next. He only wants good results for his children. He truly loves you—and it shows.

• What's one of the most difficult choices you ever had to make? Describe the scenario:

_____

_____

_____

_____

_____

_____

• The chapter includes the well-known story of Jonah. The entire book is only four chapters long, so take time to reread it. To make it even fresher, try reading it in a different translation or paraphrase. We get very accustomed to our own Bible—and that's good! But sometimes seeing the words in an alternate version can be quite stimulating and helpful. When you're finished, write down two or three observations from Jonah that are new insights for you.

_____

_____

_____

_____

_____

_____

• In Jonah 3:1, it says the word of the Lord came to Jonah "a second time." How does that relate to a Second Wind in your life?

_____

_____

_____

_____

- The story of Nelson and Judy Padgett is a testament to making the right choices even when it seems strange. What in this account struck you most significantly? Why?

_____

_____

_____

_____

_____

_____

- Spend some time in prayer. Ask God for the integrity necessary to keep your word, even when it hurts, as it says in Psalm 15. Ask him for a Second Wind in your life.

- What is the most important truth you gleaned from this chapter?

_____

_____

_____

_____

- Based on what you read in this chapter, how can *you* get a Second Wind?

_____

_____

_____

_____

_____

On Coping with the Unfairness of Others

Thomas à Kempis (c. 1380–1471)

A German mystic and spiritual director, Thomas à Kempis lived at the same time as Johann Gutenberg, inventor of modern printing. Nevertheless, Thomas worked as a copyist and is said to have copied the whole Bible by hand at least four times. This excerpt comes from his famous book The Imitation of Christ.

Those things which a man is not strong enough to put right in himself or in others, he should endure patiently until God ordains otherwise. Consider that it is perhaps better so for your testing and your patience, without which our merits are not to be highly valued. Nevertheless you should pray about such hindrances, that God may see fit to help you, that you may be able to bear them gently.

If someone, though admonished once or twice, does not comply, do not strive with him, but commit it all to God, that his will may be done, and his honour shown in all his servants. He knows well how to change evil into good. Try hard to be patient in tolerating others' faults and infirmities of whatsoever kind, because you too have much which must be tolerated by others. If you cannot make yourself as you wish, how will you be able to fashion another to your liking? We are glad to see others made perfect, and yet do not correct our own faults.

We want others to be strictly corrected, but do not wish to be corrected ourselves. The wide licence of others displeases us, and yet we do not wish that we ourselves should be denied what we desire. We want others to be bound by rules, and yet by no means do we suffer ourselves to be more restricted. So therefore it is obvious how seldom we assess our neighbor as we assess ourselves. If all men were perfect, what then should we have to tolerate from others for God's sake?

But now God has so ordained it that we should each learn to bear the other's burdens, for no one is without fault, no one without a burden, no one self-sufficient, no one wise enough for himself; but it behoves us to bear with one another, console one another, equally to help, instruct and admonish. Of what worth a man is, appears best in a time of adversity, for circumstances do not make a man frail, but they do show the kind of man he is.[1]

CHAPTER 6

WHEN IT CAN'T GET ANY WORSE

Bill Freitag carefully locked himself inside his Aurora, Illinois, house that Saturday morning and spread out newspapers on his kitchen table to begin his gun cleaning. His fourteen-year-old son, Chris, was conveniently spending the weekend at a friend's house down the street. No one else was around.

Bill arranged the pieces of his cleaning kit on the paper, then took the .357 Magnum in his hand to open the cylinder. He looked at the waiting bullet. Everything was ready. By the time someone came upon the scene of this "accident," the stabbing ache in his soul would be gone at last.

The telephone rang just then, and he jumped. *Who could that be?* he wondered.

It was Dave, the cousin of a coworker out at the Caterpillar plant. He wanted to ask something about getting into community theater, which was an avocation of Bill's.

"Yeah, some auditions and rehearsals are coming up," said the thirty-four-year-old nervously. "I'll get back to you on that."

"Okay," Dave replied.

"Uh, Dave," Bill continued, "I just want you to know that in the short period of time I've known you, you've been a good friend to me. I just wanted you to know that."

There was a chuckle on the other end of the line. "Oh, aren't we getting sentimental!" Dave replied.

"No, I just wanted to say that. I've got to go now—gotta take care of some stuff. Bye, Dave." Bill hung up the receiver.

Turning back to his weapon on the table, he picked up the bullet again with his left hand, inserted it into the chamber, and then closed the cylinder. He spun the cylinder to the notch where the bullet was, pulled back the firing hammer—and then laid the gun back down on the table.

This is it, he said to himself. *There's no going back. I have to make the pain stop. Have I covered all the bases?* He looked around the kitchen one last time, feeling very detached, almost as if watching himself in a movie.

He picked up the gun again. He had fired it many times on the shooting range and knew how sensitive the trigger was. Holding the gun now in both hands, he pointed the barrel toward his chest and hooked his thumb into the trigger guard. He took a deep breath.

"I'm sorry, but there's no other way," he said aloud, closing his eyes as he pushed against the trigger.

He waited for the blast.

Nothing happened. No click, no loud report, nothing at all. Bill opened his eyes and stared at his weapon. Why hadn't it fired?

He opened the chamber, removed the bullet, and examined everything again. All parts seemed to be in working order. He reassembled everything, turned the barrel toward his chest one more time, closed his eyes, pushed against the trigger with his thumb…and again no response.

CHRISTMAS COLLAPSE

What had driven Bill to this desperate moment was the dramatic crash of his marriage to Lenore, whom he had met in a nightclub some thirteen years before. After a whirlwind courtship, they had married. Chris, Bill's son from an earlier marriage, was there of course, and in time two more sons were born, Bryce and Adam.

This was turning out to be a rockier road than Bill had expected when he was growing up in Saint Paul's Lutheran Church as the grandson of stable Austrian immigrants. He had even gone through parochial school up to high school and felt he had a spiritual foundation. His job at Caterpillar as a ferrous operator processing steel for heavy machinery was secure. But on the home front, the metal seemed to be crumbling.

"After both deliveries of the boys," he remembers, "Lenore suffered a chemical imbalance that made life difficult. She was hospitalized for psychiatric treatment both times. Counseling seemed to help somewhat, but we began drifting apart. I began feeling like 'Who is she anyway?' and she felt the same about me."

This dragged on for several years, until Christmastime 1983, when Bryce and Adam were seven and six years old. Suddenly Lenore took her two sons one day and fled to a women's shelter. She was advised there that she did not qualify to stay unless she was a victim of some kind of abuse. There was no evidence of physical harm, but she alleged mental abuse, and so Bill was notified by the center that he must stay away from the premises.

"We had the boys' Christmas presents already bought and wrapped, waiting in their bedrooms," Bill remembers. "I was absolutely distraught. *What am I going to do? They think Dad has just abandoned them, and it's not true!* I kept saying to myself." Every time he would walk past the young boys' bedroom, his heart would break all over again.

One afternoon Chris, now a middle-school student, called his father at work. "Dad! Bryce and Adam are at their school across the street. I just saw them out the window!"

Bill immediately got his boss's permission to leave his shift and headed to the school, arriving as the day was ending. He raced down the hallway to find Lenore and the two young ones preparing to leave.

"Hello, Lenore," he said in a guarded tone. "Could I see my sons?"

A terrified look crossed the woman's face.

Bill tried to calm her. "It's okay—you can stand right nearby. I just want them to know that I'm still here for them and I love them."

The boys began jabbering. "Dad! How come you're not with us?"

Bill tried to explain. Turning to his wife, he said, "Can I at least get their Christmas presents to them?"

"I'll think about that and get back to you," she replied.

All too soon Lenore announced they must leave. As she walked them down the school corridor, the boys kept looking back over their shoulders saying, "Isn't Dad coming with us? I want Dad, I want Dad!" Bill stood watching them, choking back the sobs.

He went back to the quiet house that day and closed the boys' bedroom door so he wouldn't have to face the aching void. Somehow he made it through the holidays, although his mental anguish kept him awake many nights. The rest of the winter dragged on with attorney visits, wrangling about access rights, and mounting expense.

Bill had been seeking to buy the house they were renting, and the landlord had said he was willing to sell. Now Bill's desire to show stability made this desire even more important if there was going to be a custody battle in court. But the landlord kept stalling for some reason.

Then came the day when the man suddenly announced, "Well, actually, I need cash up-front, so I've decided to sell to somebody else. In fact, you have thirty days to get out of the house."

Says Bill, "I had always prided myself in having some semblance of control in my life. Now, one by one, things were floating further and further away. I felt as though I was spiraling down the drain."

He appealed to his family for financial help to keep up the legal battle.

His sister and brother-in-law, who lived just a few doors away, declined, pleading money problems of their own at the time.

He began scouting for apartments to rent. One after another he had to turn away, either because the rent was too high or the neighborhood wouldn't be good for his sons. "Everything I was trying to do seemed to fail. I said to God, 'Why am I being punished? What's going on here? What have I done to deserve all this?'" God seemed silent in reply.

"I felt lost, confused, alone, and frightened. I was scared out of my mind. My life was like a saltine cracker in somebody's hand that was squeezed too hard. It was just crumbling away.

"That is what brought me to the point of saying to myself, *That's it— I can't deal with this anymore. I have to make the pain stop. With my life insurance, I'm worth more to my family dead than I am alive anyway.*"

And so the suicide plan was hatched. It was now late March 1984.

A Lamp for the Darkness

At the instant the .357 Magnum refused to fire the second time, there was a noise near the front door. Bill's head jerked up—*How could anyone be in this house when I locked all the doors?*—and was stunned to see his mother, who lived nearby.

"William!" she cried, staring at the gun still in his hands. "What are you doing?!"

He looked back into his mother's anguished eyes for a moment. Then he gingerly turned the gun around, eased the hammer back down, opened up the chamber, and removed the bullet. Setting everything on the table, Bill dissolved in a flood of tears and remorse. "I'm sorry, God, I'm so sorry!" he wailed. "I had no right to do this. Please take me back—I didn't mean it. Please forgive me!"

His mother, a widow, had gotten an alarming phone call from Dave, saying she ought to go check on her son. She had arrived to find the door not only unlocked but standing open.

Now she came to put her arms around him as she instinctively began to blame herself. "Oh, Bill, Bill! What did I do? What did I do to bring this on?"

"Mom, it's not you," he answered. "It's never been anything you've done. I just couldn't cope with everything."

The tears flowed for a long time. That night Bill prayed again for forgiveness and guidance. "Lord, in the Bible you said you would be a lamp for my feet. Show me. Lead me. I have nothing left inside me—I'm all used up. Fill me. Do with me what you wish. I can't handle life on my own, so show me your will."

Sometime the next week, after Bill's head had cleared, he took the gun to a pistol range. He loaded up the chambers, cocked the hammer back, pointed it at the target, and lightly squeezed the trigger as he had done so many times before.

The revolver fired perfectly.

SOMETHING TO LIVE FOR

—Bill—

When I met Bill eighteen years later while I was speaking at the suburban Chicago church he and his wife, Julie, attend, I found a man full of life and energy. Now in his early fifties, he is still active in drama. The real passion of his life, however, is to talk to others about the Lord, not only at church but in his everyday life throughout the week.

He doesn't tell his personal story often, knowing that some would find it too astounding to believe. Instead, he focuses on what Christ can do for those who are at their lowest point. To a childhood friend who asked why he was talking about "religion" so much these days, he replied, "Gary, you and I know all about metalworking, right? To get the strongest steel, we have to put it through the forge. We have to purge out the impurities, to temper it, and to reshape it.

"Well, people are no different. God puts us through the fire in order to purge us of the bad stuff. That's how we become more useful."

Bill Freitag is an example of what the famous Corrie ten Boom, Dutch survivor of Nazi death camps, once said, "There is no pit so deep that He is not deeper still." Those who are at the absolute bottom of their lives, drained of all hope and promise, are still eligible for a merciful God to intervene. It may not be as dramatic as God's stopping a lethal bullet, but it can still make the difference between life and death, joy and utter despair.

That is what happened to the man lying beside the Pool of Bethesda, as told in the New Testament (John 5). He had been paralyzed for thirty-eight years: destitute, unemployable, alone in the world. Hopelessness had set in a long time ago. Days dragged by slowly, one after another. The idea that life could ever be anything different or better was not even on his horizon. *Hope* was a word for teenagers, for children, for anyone but him.

The only thing even close to hope in his life was actually a shred of folklore. Superstition had it that once in a great while, the waters of the pool would be rippled by an angel's touch, and whoever got into the water first thereafter would be healed. Was it really true or just a myth? Anyway, he was immobile, and therefore he wasn't going to win any race. As he explained to Jesus, "Sir, I have no one to help me into the pool when the water is stirred. While I am trying to get in, someone else goes down ahead of me" (verse 7).

This man was truly stuck in the basement of life. No chance for a brighter future as far as he could tell.

The stranger from Nazareth came along one day and asked a few questions. He found out the man's background—how long he had been lying there, how impossible his situation was. And then Jesus came out with a question that sounded almost silly:

"Do you want to get well?" (verse 6).

What Jesus was doing was moving the focus from the external to the internal. He was probing the man's inner attitude. Did he really *want* to get better? If so, how much did he want it?

The Lord asks the same of us today. When we are down and discouraged and despondent, he wants to know the state of our heart and mind. Is there any desire to see the Second Wind come blowing into our lives, or do we consider our fate to be sealed?

The invalid by the pool immediately told Jesus how unlikely it was that he would ever get into the pool first. In other words, his attention immediately swerved back to the external. Other people were at fault. He placed the blame for his condition on what someone else was or wasn't doing.

I have met more than a few people who say, in essence, "Do you want to know what my problem is? It's my spouse!"

Or "my kids."

Or "my boss."

Or "my neighbors."

The difficulty is *out there*. Not me. It's *them*.

Life and management expert Stephen Covey writes, "As long as you believe the problem is 'out there'—that's the problem."

Jesus did not even debate the issue with the invalid man. He simply went straight for the divine answer. "Get up! Pick up your mat and walk," he ordered (verse 8). Within seconds, the man was dizzily vertical, taking his first steps in a brand-new world.

He didn't even know who had intervened in his life. When the religious leaders quizzed him on how this miracle had occurred, "the man who was healed had no idea who it was, for Jesus had slipped away into the crowd" (verse 13). Only later did he get the rest of the facts.

God loves us right now, in spite of our depression and all the other ills that engulf us. He would like for us to *want* to get well, to *want* to be raised up to a whole new level. But sometimes, in his mercy he doesn't even wait for us to figure that out. He just steps in and unleashes his power on our behalf.

He knows there are far better days waiting in our future. When we think things cannot get any worse, he shows us they can be better than our wildest dreams. He's that kind of marvelous God.

PERSONAL JOURNAL

• When you read Bill Freitag's story, what was your first thought?

_____

_____

_____

• The title of this chapter is "When It Can't Get Any Worse." Is that an accurate description of your life right now? Describe your life in two or three sentences. Or, if your life is in a better place, think back to when it was difficult, and write a two-sentence description.

_____

_____

_____

_____

_____

_____

• When Jesus asked the paralyzed man if he wanted to get well, he was digging deep inside to the man's attitude. In the same way, do _you_ really want a Second Wind in your life? What is there about a Second Wind that frightens you? What would keep you from going for a Second Wind in your life? Jot down your answers.

_____

_____

_____

_____

_____

• One of the most creative ways to interact personally with the Scriptures is to rewrite the verses in your own words, or paraphrasing. One advantage is that it forces you to personalize the text. Paraphrase John 5:1-14.

_____

_____

_____

_____

_____

_____

_____

_____

_____

_____

_____

• The man at the pool blamed others for his inability to be healed. Do you ever have the tendency to blame others for the difficulties in your life? Who tends to get the blame? Why do you do it? How can you avoid falling into this trap in the future?

_____

_____

_____

_____

_____

_____

- What is the most important truth you gleaned from this chapter?

_____

_____

_____

_____

- Based on what you read in this chapter, how can *you* get a Second Wind?

_____

_____

_____

_____

_____

_____

ON SURRENDER AND FAITH

Hannah Whitall Smith (1832–1911)

A warmly welcomed speaker throughout both the United States and England in the late nineteenth century, Hannah Whitall Smith, along with her husband, emphasized a spiritual life that rose above drudgery and exertion. The following excerpt is taken from chapter 4 of her classic book The Christian's Secret of a Happy Life, *first published in 1875.*

[The] blessed life must not be looked upon in any sense as an attainment, but as an obtainment. We cannot earn it, we cannot climb up to it, we cannot win it; we can do nothing but ask for it and receive it. It is the gift of God in Christ Jesus. And where a thing is a gift, the only course left for the receiver is to take it and thank the giver.

We never say of a gift, "See to what I have attained," and boast of our skill and wisdom in having attained it; but we say, "See what has been given to me," and boast of the love and wealth and generosity of the giver....

In order, therefore, to enter into a practical experience of this interior life, the soul must be in a receptive attitude, fully recognizing the fact that it is God's gift in Christ Jesus, and that it cannot be gained by any efforts or works of our own. This will simplify the matter exceedingly; and the only thing left to be considered then, will be to discover upon whom God bestows this gift, and how they are to receive it. To this I would answer, in short, that He can bestow it only upon the fully consecrated soul, and that it is to be received by faith.

Consecration is the first thing,—not in any legal sense, not in order to purchase or deserve the blessing, but to remove the difficulties out of the way and make it possible for God to bestow it. In order for a lump of clay to be made into a beautiful vessel, it must be entirely abandoned to the potter, and must lie passive in his hands. And similarly, in order for a soul to be made into a vessel unto God's honor, "sanctified, and meet for the master's use, and prepared unto every good work," [2 Timothy 2:21, KJV] it must be utterly abandoned to Him, and must lie passive in His hands. This is manifest at the first glance.

I was once trying to explain to a physician who had charge of a large hospital, the necessity and meaning of consecration, but he seemed unable to understand. At last I said to him, "Suppose, in going your rounds among your patients, you should meet with one man who entreated you earnestly to take his case under your especial care in order to cure him, but who should at the same time refuse to tell you all his symptoms or to take all your prescribed remedies, and should say to you, 'I am quite willing to follow your directions as to certain things, because they commend themselves to my mind as good, but in other matters I prefer judging for myself, and following my own directions.' What would you do in such a case?" I asked.

"Do!" he replied with indignation,—"Do! I would soon leave such a man as that to his own care. For, of course," he added, "I could do nothing for him unless he would put his whole case into my hands without any reserves, and would obey my directions implicitly."

"It is necessary, then," I said, "for doctors to be obeyed, if they are to have any chance to cure their patient?"

"Implicitly obeyed!" was his emphatic reply.

"And that is consecration," I continued. "God must have the whole case put into His hands without any reserves, and His directions must be implicitly followed."

"I see it," he exclaimed; "I see it! And I will do it. God shall have His own way with me from henceforth."

To some minds perhaps the word "abandonment" might express this idea better than the word "consecration." But whatever word we use, we mean an entire surrender of the whole being to God,—spirit, soul, and body placed under His absolute control, for Him to do with us just what He pleases.... We mean the giving up of all liberty of choice....

To a soul ignorant of God, this may look hard; but to those who know Him, it is the happiest and most restful of lives.... A great many Christians seem practically to think that all their Father in heaven wants is a chance to make them miserable and to take away all their blessings; and they imagine, poor souls, that if they hold on to things in their own will, they can hinder Him from doing this. I am ashamed to write the words, yet we must face a fact which is making wretched hundreds of lives....

...I beg of you not to look at [consecration] as a hard and stern demand. You must do it gladly, thankfully, enthusiastically. You must go in on what I call the privilege side of consecration; and I can assure you, from the universal testimony of all who have tried it, that you will find it the happiest place you have ever entered yet.

Faith is the next thing after surrender.... I suppose most Christians understand this principle in reference to the matter of their forgiveness. They know that the forgiveness of sins through Jesus might have been preached to them forever, but it would never really have become theirs until they believed this preaching, and claimed the forgiveness as their own. But when it comes to living the Christian life, they lose sight of this principle, and think that, having been saved by faith, they are now to live by works and efforts; and instead of continuing to *receive,* they are now to begin to *do....* And yet it is plainly declared that, "*as* we have received Christ Jesus the Lord, *so* we are to walk in Him" [see Colossians 2:6]....

I mean all this, of course, experimentally and practically.... No faith that is exercised in the future tense amounts to anything…. No faith that looks for a future deliverance from the power of sin, will ever lead a soul into the life we are describing. The enemy delights in this future faith, for he knows it is powerless to accomplish any practical results. But he trembles and flees when the soul of the believer dares to claim a present deliverance, and to reckon itself *now* to be free from his power….

A man was obliged to descend into a deep well by sliding down a fixed rope which was supposed to be of ample length. But to his dismay he came to the end of it before his feet had touched the bottom. He had not the strength to climb up again, and to let go and drop seemed to him but to be dashed to pieces in the depths below.

He held on until his strength was utterly exhausted, and then dropped, as he thought, to his death. He fell—just three inches—and found himself safe on the rock bottom.

Are you afraid to take this step? Does it seem too sudden, too much like a leap in the dark? Do you not know that the step of faith always "falls on the seeming void, but finds the rock beneath?" If ever you are to enter this glorious land…you must sooner or later step into the brimming waters, for there is no other path; and to do it now, may save you months and even years of disappointment and grief.[1]

CHAPTER 7

FACING GIANTS

—Bill—

I always enjoy telling audiences about my glory days as a member of the legendary 1972 "Perfect Season" Miami Dolphins, the only professional football team to go an entire year without losing. From the opening 20–10 win at Kansas City to the crowning victory over the Washington Redskins in Super Bowl VII, it was an awesome experience.

Listeners today observe my age and my bulk, and they can well imagine how, Sunday after Sunday, we mowed down every opponent who dared to face us. The roster was an assemblage of talent for the ages.

Fullback Larry Csonka piled up 1,117 yards while, over the same season, running back Mercury Morris got another 1,000—the first rushing duo in the NFL to do this.

When quarterback Bob Griese went down in the fifth game with a broken leg, "Old Bones" Earl Morrall stepped in to keep the streak going.

Meanwhile, middle linebacker Nick Buoniconti and the rest of his No-Name Defense held opponents to a season total of only eight touchdowns.

Three times we shut out the other team altogether, including a 52–0 shellacking of New England to give coach Don Shula his one hundredth win.

And I was a young college student who sold programs each week in the Orange Bowl's nosebleed section.

This was serious business, let me assure you. We had to show up at eight in the morning to get our supply. The veteran salesmen, of course, laid claim to the plum spots outside where customers would come from the parking lots, while we rookies got to huff and puff up and down the bleachers in search of leftovers. But at least we were inside the stadium, where we could watch the game for free.

I still remember the last home game of the year. In those days, television had nothing like today's studio halftime shows with scores and highlights from all around the league; our big splash that day was to be the Punt, Pass & Kick finals for kids ages six to twelve. After the pros had finished their practices that morning, the television producers brought out these dozens of little boys for rehearsal. Dressed in their miniature Dolphins helmets and shirts, they excitedly went through their drills, learning where to throw the ball and when to run off the field. We program vendors watched with amusement from the top of the still-empty stands.

One cute little guy was so short that, even in his miniature gear, he basically looked like a helmet with cleats. As the rehearsal ended and everyone else moved toward the sidelines, we could see him intentionally hanging back, until soon he had his dream: a pro football field all to himself. None of the adults seemed to notice.

He quickly began his fantasy. In the center of the field, he squatted like a quarterback, squeaked out his snap count, and took the imaginary hike. Fading back into the pocket, he soon began to scramble. Side to side he ran, desperately looking for an imaginary receiver. At last, he heaved a Hail Mary pass.

At that moment, of course, a miracle took place: The kid morphed into a wide receiver. He hauled in his own pass and began feinting his way through hordes of phantom defenders toward the end zone. There he spiked the ball and went into an exuberant dance—while a hundred of us program salesmen jumped up and loudly cheered from the stadium rim, shocking the boy to death.

SMALL BODY, BIG HEART

I love telling that story, and I usually go on to say, "Now what if I made one little change? What if I told you that Nick Buoniconti and the fearsome Dolphins defenders actually *were* on the field at the moment...and still the six-year-old kid scored a touchdown on them? Wouldn't that be an amazing tale?"

That is basically what happened in the Old Testament (1 Samuel 17) the day young David fought Goliath.

It's the quintessential story of courage against all odds. Everybody's heard it, I know. But its familiarity ought not to disqualify its point, which is that when we face overwhelming threats to our very life and limb, God can give us the audacity to stand and conquer.

The giant was "over nine feet tall," says verse 4. When I speak, I often dramatize this by climbing up on top of a three-foot stool. I nearly break my neck, but the crowd loves it.

Goliath had "a bronze helmet on his head and wore a coat of scale armor of bronze weighing five thousand shekels" (verse 5)—anywhere from 148 to 200 pounds. My somewhat corny illustration of this is to have an adult man from the audience (hopefully not too large) come jump onto my back.

Goliath's armor probably weighed more than David did!

The giant's spear was like the main rod on a loom (my prop for this is a microphone stand), and the spearhead alone weighed seventeen to twenty pounds. Yet Goliath was prepared to throw it with force.

Besides all this hardware, the man had a very big mouth. He intimidated, he mocked, he trash-talked. "This day I defy the ranks of Israel! Give me a man and let us fight each other" (verse 10). He held no respect whatever for David or David's God.

How many times has the wind been taken out of your sails by the hot air coming from a giant? Whether a huge corporation or a nasty prosecuting attorney or a threatening family member, the power of words can immobilize us if we let it. We can, like the Israelite troops, huddle in our tents and put our hands over our ears.

Not David. He boldly said that he didn't much care what Goliath thought of him. He wasn't impressed with his size or his gear. He was going to take the guy on, regardless.

You wouldn't expect such a statement from one so young. The previous chapter of 1 Samuel tells us he was the last-born of eight sons—the "baby" of the family. If you believe in the birth-order hypothesis, you know that the youngest are said to be laid-back underachievers, fun lovers, even jokesters. That's their alleged way of dealing with the inferiority they feel toward their older, taller siblings.

David was a part-time shepherd and part-time musician. Neither one of those professions is especially warlike or heroic. How much bravery does it take to strum a harp?

Yet God saw something different in David. Through the prophet Samuel he said in what has become a famous scripture, "The LORD does not look at the things man looks at. Man looks at the outward appearance, but the LORD looks at the heart" (16:7).

That's what it's all about when facing tough circumstances: *heart.* A résumé doesn't tell you much about what the person's heart is like. For all of us in challenging environments, the truth is this: No matter what you look like physically, no matter who you're up against in your workplace or your neighborhood, no matter your health, socioeconomic status, or race, whether you are considered "too young" or "too old"—it's all about heart.

That, in fact, is the origin of the word *courage*. The French word for *heart* is *cœur;* the Spanish is *corazón*. Courage comes from a strong heart, deep within a person. When we give our hearts to God, he infuses them with supernatural courage.

The reason I talk about this perhaps most famous Bible story of all is that David shows dramatic initiative. After twenty-five verses of people basically wimping out, this young man says in 1 Samuel 17:26, "What will be done for the man who kills this Philistine and removes this disgrace from Israel? Who is this uncircumcised Philistine that he should defy the armies of the living God?"

He is clearly setting out to do something that's never been done before. He isn't going to wait for Goliath to go away or for somebody older and more trained to step up. He is going to press forward himself.

This promptly earns him a barrage of criticism. His oldest brother, in typical older-sibling style, makes a crack about his motives. "Why have you come down here? And with whom did you leave those few sheep in the desert? I know how conceited you are and how wicked your heart is; you came down only to watch the battle" (verse 28). David is not dissuaded in the least. Within minutes he is talking to King Saul about his intent to make Goliath shut up. The king tells the young man he's crazy. The giant has been training longer than David has been living, he observes.

David rebuts the criticism with facts. He tells the king how he handled vicious lions and bears while tending his father's sheep. Soon the king yields to the young man's desire, probably saying to himself, *Well, nobody else is volunteering, so maybe we can use this kid to see what the Big Guy's got.*

A well-known psychological test called the Myers-Briggs Type Indicator distinguishes between people who are primarily *thinkers* and those who are primarily *feelers*. I confess I'm more of the second stripe. We feelers tend to struggle with criticism, whereas thinkers are more objective. They process it quickly, decide whether it's valid or not, and move on.

David, though a sensitive musician, showed great maturity here in pushing through the criticism. His proactive heart would not be denied.

Next came the "helpful suggestion" from Saul about using traditional armor. The scene quickly turned ridiculous. David had to pursue his calling in his own style, which for him was to be lightly armed with only a slingshot and five stones.

What is your *specific* calling here on earth? Why has God allowed you to be here? Beyond the general mandates of Scripture to love one another, to share the Good News, to stand for justice, and so forth...what will be absent from the world when you finally pass away?

This passage vividly tells us to do what God wants *us* to do. As we follow through in our own personalized style, we will be victorious.

I find it interesting that the New Testament passage about the armor of God leads off with a preface that says, "Be strong *in the Lord* and in his mighty power" (Ephesians 6:10, emphasis added). Only then does the writer proceed to name and describe six different pieces of equipment: the belt of truth, the shield of faith, the helmet of salvation, etc. In other words, victory is not really about the armor; it's not how tall I am or how heavy my spearhead. It is about taking action *in the Lord.*

You can win with even a pebble if God is in it. Others may sneer and think you're only a miniature. It doesn't matter. The Second Wind comes to propel those who are courageous and proactive.

HANGING TOUGH

A couple of hours' drive east of me lives a couple named Don and Kay Bennett. Theirs is the story of facing huge challenges in the California real estate market, sometimes soaring to the heights and other times nearly going bankrupt. Don set a goal early in their marriage to be a millionaire by age forty, and he succeeded. His private life, however, was a cauldron of stress and unfaithfulness to Kay, which pushed her to reach out for spiritual help. That is how she became a Christian—and began taking her reluctant husband to church as well.

He listened each week but didn't change. "I was a double-minded man," he now says, paraphrasing James 1:8, "unstable in all my ways."

Not until April 1984 did an employee of Don's, a Mexican American woman, ask him straight-out what was really wrong. He told her that God couldn't possibly forgive his many sins. She promptly reached for her Bible and read the story of the adulterous King David being confronted by the prophet Nathan. After painting the bleak picture, she said, "But even so, look what God said about this man in the book of Acts: 'I have found David son of Jesse a man after my own heart; he will do everything I want him to do'" (13:22).

In that instant, Don Bennett finally got it. He understood the depth of God's forgiveness. He realized he could be accepted by a holy God after all, if he would only repent and submit. He made a dramatic turn in his life, reconciled with Kay, began devouring Christian books, and rejoiced in his new life in Christ.

The next five years were great, both at home and in his business. He sold one firm, used the proceeds to expand his development projects, and in early 1989 bought a prime lot in upscale La Quinta (southeast of Palm Desert) to build their dream home of fifty-eight hundred square feet. By that fall, Don had some 7.5 million dollars' worth of construction under way, mostly in the San Francisco Bay area, to be resold.

Some readers will remember that 1989 was the year the West Coast real estate bubble started to sag. "I sensed a turn in the market," says Don. "I soon realized I was in trouble. Over the next months, I had to sell every piece of property I owned—at depressed prices. But even that triggered capital gains taxes, which I struggled to pay."

In 1991 the Bennetts moved into the La Quinta house and immediately put it on the market. Nothing happened. Meanwhile, three different "friends" who owed Don a total of $750,000 declared bankruptcy. His income plummeted.

"Okay, God, what's going on here?" Don prayed. This was not exactly the divine blessing he had assumed would accompany his turn to Christ a few years back. He began searching the Scriptures more deeply than ever before to find an anchor.

He memorized such verses as…

Trust in the LORD with all your heart
    and lean not on your own understanding;
in all your ways acknowledge him,
    and he will make your paths straight. (Proverbs 3:5-6)

A few verses later came this comment about tough times:

My son, do not despise the LORD's discipline
    and do not resent his rebuke,
because the LORD disciplines those he loves,
    as a father the son he delights in. (verses 11-12)

Says Don: "When we think about God's faithfulness, we usually equate it with deliverance from trials. That was certainly my hope at the time. But I had to learn that God is in the process of conforming us to the image of his Son; he's shaping and molding us. This doesn't mean he will always shield us from the fire; instead, he will walk through it with us.

"It definitely wasn't fun going through total financial devastation. But when I considered my relationship with God compared to wealth without Christ, there was no contest."

Don and Kay kept reading the Word of God, praying, going to church, and even tithing on what little income they had. Right after the Christmas holidays, they began sponsoring their own open-house promotions to try to liquidate their home. A couple on a bike ride, who weren't actually looking to buy, stopped by one day—and fell in love with the house. Soon a deal was worked out that included a swap of the Bennetts' large home for the other couple's smaller one. When escrow closed thirty days later, Don and Kay had less than ten dollars in their checking account.

"Shortly after our move, we began attending a small-group Bible study. Within a year, we were asked by the church to start a new one in our home. Soon the group was up to sixteen or eighteen people every Thursday night."

But two years later they still found themselves in major financial distress, with more than $250,000 worth of debt. "I worked very hard and prayed even harder," Don says. "We kept on tithing because we knew it was for our good. But eventually, we reached a point where we couldn't make the next house payment."

They were doing all the "right things"…and still no relief.

A friend brought a prospective buyer one day, who ended up paying cash for their house. Don and Kay swallowed hard as they moved out and rented a sixteen-hundred-square-foot condo. "Here I was—the big-shot real estate broker and developer—paying rent!" he says with chagrin. "I remembered that several years earlier I had looked at this particular floor plan and said I'd never live in such a place. Yet there we were, utterly humbled."

Eventually, on a memorable day in November 1995, Don was driving down a street in his neighborhood when he prayed in his car, "Lord, you've been faithful to me. You've allowed Kay and me to maintain our credit and honor all our commitments somehow. I'm very grateful. And Lord, we've been faithful to you too. We've tithed all through these six difficult years. Now, Lord…would you open the floodgates? Would you allow us to prosper once again?" He pled for God's smile after so long.

From that very day Don's business began to blossom. He started getting calls and referrals out of nowhere. Income began to climb steadily. After four years of recovery, they were able to buy a house once more.

As of this writing, the Bennetts are still doing well, both materially and spiritually. "As I look back," he says when he speaks to groups, "I see the love and wisdom of God. I see how he pruned me and caused me to grow in him. I see how he reshaped my priorities and taught me what it meant to truly trust him. I give him credit each time I make a new transaction."

Personally speaking, I think the new prosperity has some connection to Don and Kay's diligent work all through the hard times. They never quit. They kept stepping out in courage, doing what they knew to be right as God's children, giving time and money to the Lord's work just because they knew they should. They made every business move they could think of and covered the whole effort in serious prayer. Eventually, God's second outpouring began to flow in their direction.

Another scripture that Don has memorized is Isaiah 43:1-3,5:

Fear not, for I have redeemed you;
    I have summoned you by name; you are mine.
When you pass through the waters,
    I will be with you;
and when you pass through the rivers,
    they will not sweep over you.
When you walk through the fire,

you will not be burned;

the flames will not set you ablaze.

For I am the LORD, your God....

Do not be afraid, for I am with you.

That's his promise to those who follow him proactively and single-mindedly—with all their *hearts*.

- David was described in this chapter as a part-time shepherd, part-time musician, who was the baby of his family. When you think about this description in relation to your life, what is it about David with which you identify?

_____

_____

_____

_____

_____

- Who or what are the Goliaths in your life right now? If more than one, list them in order from biggest to smallest.

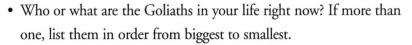

The Giants in My Life

_____

_____

_____

_____

_____

- Have you ever been humbled by the Lord, like the time Don and Kay Bennett had to move from their big, beautiful home to a more modest house? What were some of the lessons God taught you through that experience?

_____

_____

_____

_____

_____

_____

• Can you think of other characters in the Bible who were proactive?
  Use the names below to jog your thinking. How did each of these
  characters take the initiative in their life?

  Bible Character   _How They Were Proactive_

  Abraham

  Joseph

  Moses

  Joshua

  Ruth

  Solomon

  Esther

  John the Baptist

  Peter

  Paul

• How can _you_ become more proactive in your life? What is it that
  you know God wants you to do, yet you're holding back? How
  would God's Second Wind be helpful in taking the initiative with
  his power? Where is God asking you to be courageous?

  _____

  _____

  _____

  _____

  _____

_____

_____

- What is the most important truth you gleaned from this chapter?

_____

_____

_____

_____

_____

- Based on what you read in this chapter, how can *you* get a Second Wind?

_____

_____

_____

_____

ON OVERCOMING

Dwight L. Moody (1837–99)

America's premier evangelist in the nineteenth century, Dwight L. Moody was never formally ordained as a minister. Yet he traveled more than a million miles and spoke to more than a hundred million people, his plain explanation of the gospel drawing wide response. His legacy still thrives through the Moody Bible Institute in Chicago.

In these excerpts from a sermon entitled "The Christian's Warfare," he speaks bluntly about the reality of facing spiritual battles.

When I was converted I made this mistake: I thought the battle was already mine, the victory already won, the crown already in my grasp. I thought that old things had passed away, that all things had become new; that my old corrupt nature, the Adam life, was gone. But I found out, after serving Christ for a few months, that conversion was only like enlisting in the army, that there was a battle on hand, and that if I was to get a crown, I had to work for it and fight for it....

It is like this: when a man enters the army, he is a member of the army the moment he enlists; he is just as much a member as a man who has been in the army ten or twenty years. But enlisting is one thing, and participating in a battle another. Young converts are like those just enlisted.

It is folly for any man to attempt to fight in his own strength. The world, the flesh and the devil are too much for any man. But if we are linked to Christ by faith, and He is formed in us the hope of glory, then we shall get the victory over every enemy. It is believers who are the over-comers. "Thanks be unto God, which always causeth us to triumph in

Christ" [2 Corinthians 2:14]. Through Him we shall be more than conquerors.

I wouldn't think of talking to unconverted men about overcoming the world, for it is utterly impossible. They might as well try to cut down the American forest with their penknives. But a good many Christian people make this mistake: they think the battle is already fought and won. They have an idea that all they have to do is to put the oars down in the bottom of the boat, and the current will drift them into the ocean of God's eternal love. But we have to cross the current. We have to learn how to watch and fight, and how to overcome. The battle is only just commenced. The Christian life [is] a conflict and a warfare, and the quicker we find it out the better....

Now many a young believer is discouraged and disheartened when he realizes this warfare. He begins to think that God has forsaken him, that Christianity is not all that it professes to be. But he should rather regard it as an encouraging sign. No sooner has a soul escaped from his snare than the great Adversary takes steps to ensnare it again.... The fiercest attacks are made on the strongest forts, and the fiercer the battle the young believer is called on to wage, the surer evidence it is of the work of the Holy Spirit in his heart. God will not desert him in his time of need, any more than He deserted His people of old when they were hard pressed by their foes....

Everything human in this world fails. Every man the moment he takes his eye off God, has failed. Every man has been a failure at some period of his life.... Peter was noted for his boldness, and a little maid scared him nearly out of his wits. As soon as she spoke to him, he began to tremble, and he swore that he didn't know Christ. I have often said to myself that I'd like to have been there on the day of Pentecost alongside of that maid when she saw Peter preaching.

"Why," I suppose she said, "what has come over that man? He was afraid of *me* only a few weeks ago, and now he stands up before all Jerusalem and charges these very Jews with the murder of Jesus."…

…Every dart Satan can fire at us we can quench by faith. By faith we can overcome the Evil One. To fear is to have more faith in your antagonist than in Christ.

Some of the older people can remember when our [Civil] [W]ar broke out. Secretary Seward, who was Lincoln's Secretary of State—a long-headed and shrewd politician—prophesied that the war would be over in ninety days; and young men in thousands and hundreds of thousands came forward and volunteered to go down to Dixie and whip the South. They thought they would be back in ninety days; but the war lasted four years, and cost about half a million of lives. What was the matter? Why, the South was a good deal stronger than the North supposed. Its strength was underestimated.

Jesus Christ makes no mistake of that kind. When He enlists a man in His service, He shows him the dark side; He lets him know that he must live a life of self-denial. If a man is not willing to go to heaven by the way of Calvary, he cannot go at all.… Do not think that you will have no battles if you follow the Nazarene, because many battles are before you. Yet if I had ten thousand lives, Jesus Christ should have every one of them. Men do not object to a battle if they are confident that they will have victory, and, thank God, every one of us may have the victory if we will.

The reason why so many Christians fail all through life is just this— they underestimate the strength of the enemy. My dear friend, you and I have got a terrible enemy to contend with. Don't let Satan deceive you. Unless you are spiritually dead, it means warfare. Nearly everything around tends to draw us away from God. We do not step clear out of Egypt on to the throne of God. There is a wilderness journey, and there are enemies in the land.…

If you are not overcoming temptations, the world is overcoming you. Just get on your knees and ask God to help you. My dear friends, let us go to God and ask Him to search us. Let us ask Him to wake us up, and let us not think that just because we are church members we are all right. We are all wrong if we are not getting victory over sin.[1]

CHAPTER 8

YES, IT HURTS

—Bill—

A curious difference between Americans and those who live in other parts of the world is that most of us Americans just naturally assume that life ought to be pain-free. The norm, in our opinion, should *not* include suffering, crisis, difficulty, or hassle. Let the good times roll.

On the other hand, millions of people in Asia, Africa, Latin America, and even Europe wake up in the morning with the opposite assumption. They've lived through so many wars, so many economic collapses, so many plagues that they just expect more of the same—if not today, then probably tomorrow or next month or next year. Hardship is par for the course.

This is a sweeping generality, I admit. But there's more than a grain of truth in it.

Each world-view has its advantages. The first is upbeat, optimistic, and therefore looking for opportunity. The second is said to be realistic and therefore not as prone to emotional crashes when things turn out badly.

When we Americans hit a rough stretch—when illness strikes, our career goes into a stall, or a relationship breaks down—we are more prone to ask, "Why me? Hey, I deserve better than this. My life was supposed to be smooth. So what's the deal here? How did this happen to me?"

NOT IF, BUT WHEN

The man who wrote the epistle of James (he was, in fact, the half-brother of Jesus) was obviously not of our mind-set. He opened his letter right off the bat with the premise that hard times *are going to come* to everyone, and in fact they have a silver lining. His perspective is almost offensive to our ears:

> Consider it pure joy, my brothers and sisters, whenever you face
> trials of many kinds, because you know that the testing of your faith
> produces perseverance. Let perseverance finish its work so that you
> may be mature and complete, not lacking anything. (1:2-4)

Notice he didn't say "*if* you happen by some twist of bad luck to face trials." He said "whenever" you face trials. The word implies certainty—they will come. It also implies frequency—more than just once per lifetime.

Thanks a lot. Just what you always wanted for Christmas, right?

Testing should not catch us off guard. The fact that we will face difficulty is a given. In fact, it is *un*natural and *il*logical and *un*biblical to think we will breeze through life without tough times. We can count on their periodic appearances. The only question is when they will come, for how long, and how we will handle them.

Any theology is far off-base that says once you accept Christ, all your problems will melt away like a snowfall in April. Christ himself never taught that, and neither did the New Testament writers. What they did say was that we, unlike unbelievers, have access to a solution for our testings. Our hope is in Christ. We are not left to solve our problems alone.

People in distress sometimes say, "I've come to the end of my rope." The beautiful thing for a Christian is to realize it's not the end after all. In fact, we may need to admit we've been hanging on to the wrong rope! We should be clinging to God's rope, not ours. And when we do, we begin to see how the situation might work out for God's glory.

The book of James, by the way, is probably the earliest book of the New Testament era, written only some thirteen years after the Day of Pentecost, when the church was born. You might say James was writing to a still-adolescent church. He wanted his readers to get beyond the emotions of adolescence, to grow up, to "be mature and complete" (1:4).

To explain that more fully, he employed three words that, in English, all start with the letter *t*. One is an overarching category, and the other two are subsections of the first. It looks like this in outline form:

I. "Trials of many kinds" (verse 2). What kinds, you ask?
    A. Testings (verse 3)
    B. Temptations (verses 13-15)

A and B are not the same thing. In fact, they contrast sharply when you notice that testings are embraced as part of God's overall strategy while temptations definitely are *not* his doing. As James explains:

> When tempted, no one should say, "God is tempting me." For God
> cannot be tempted by evil, nor does he tempt anyone; but each of
> you is tempted when you are dragged away by your own evil desire
> and enticed. Then, after desire has conceived, it gives birth to sin;
> and sin, when it is full-grown, gives birth to death. (1:13-15)

Testing, suffering, trials, and difficulty may be allowed by the hand of God, but they never take the form of temptation, enticing us to sin.

Both A and B have this in common, however: They take the measure of our commitment to God. They find out what we're really made of. They push us for the true character beneath the surface.

This whole section of Scripture highlights an incredibly encouraging thing about God's nature. Verse 17 says he is "the Father of the heavenly lights, who does not change like shifting shadows." The *New American Standard Bible* renders this "with whom there is no variation." It is a reference to the precision of the solar system—the sun, moon, and outlying stars. Even in these ancient times, people had come to realize that the sun did the same thing repeatedly throughout the year. It didn't rise in the east one day and the northwest the next day. You could count on its reliability. You could make plans based on what the heavenly lights told you. You could navigate across the Mediterranean in a small boat by watching the stars. There was no variation.

So it is with the God who made the universe. He doesn't waffle. The theological term for this is God's *immutability.* His character is locked in; it's 100 percent unchangeable.

In other words, you will never catch God having a bad day. It would be totally out of character for him.

The human being you love most…the person who epitomizes reliability…who you say would never let you down in a hundred years…is still capable of hurting you sometime in your life. God, on the other hand, will never be that kind of person. You'll never call him and get a busy signal or be put on hold. Your call will never be forwarded to some other god. You will always get through. No variation.

Here is our hope for tough times! Our troubles may last longer than we would like, but the beauty is, God is always there, and he will never change. Your situations will vary; God stays the same.

We are by nature variable people. We deviate all the time from the kind of person we claim to be. A change of environment can bring out responses we never thought we would utter.

To give an extreme illustration: Imagine the classic marine drill sergeant with his crew cut, yelling at his new recruits in boot camp. *"Awrrright! I want a hundred push-ups from you bunch of so-and-sos, and I want 'em right now! Get down there in the mud! One—two—three—four! Go! Go! Go! Call out your count. I can't heeeear you!"*

He's barking right into their faces. That's his job.

Then the day ends. He signs out. He lingers to do a little extra paper-work this particular day, and as a result, he arrives home late for dinner.

He walks into the apartment. His wife is not happy. "Where have you been?! I've been holding dinner for twenty minutes! Why didn't you call me and say you'd be late?"

Our tough drill sergeant suddenly turns into Mort Meek. "I'm sorry, I'm sorry, honey," he whimpers. "I got held up. Don't hit me. I won't be late again, I promise."

That's *variation.*

Aren't you glad you never run the risk of catching God in a barking mode? He never wakes up and says, "I think I'll make all the believers do push-ups today, just for the fun of it." He never turns sarcastic with us. He never says, "You and your nitpicky little problem—don't you know I've got a whole universe to run up here? Give me a break."

No, he is always the same: mature, controlled, gracious, wise. Day after day, month after month, crisis after crisis, he's working on our maturity.

THE INTERRUPTED LECTURE

Let me illustrate this in the life of a man we met in the Chicago suburbs named Bill Rot (pronounced "rote"). He's now in his early sixties after a long and successful career in retailing. Things went well in his life for a good stretch: raised in a stable Christian home by hard-working Dutch immigrant parents, got the chance to study business at the University of

Iowa, married during his senior year, landed a job with JCPenney right out of school, eventually rose to manage a forty-million-dollar-a-year store in a major mall, bought a house in the upscale suburb of Barrington, and meanwhile became the father of four: two sons and two daughters.

"I always loved the classroom," he says with a smile. "I loved doing training for the Penney company. I dreamed about teaching in a college setting.

"One day a friend challenged me to quit talking about it and do something. So I called nearby Harper College to see if they had any openings. Next thing I knew I was an adjunct professor, teaching night courses in marketing and consumer behavior, while I kept up with my day job at the store."

Bill's expertise was soon put to additional use on the college's Retail Advisory Committee. He could not have been happier.

Then came Thursday, March 19, 1992—a day that will live in the Rot family history forever.

He had worked all day and then driven to the campus to start teaching at six. Around twenty students came in for the three-hour lecture—the typical older crowd going to night school. Bill felt fine and was enjoying the interaction as usual when "suddenly it felt like somebody was standing behind me pressing a big corkscrew into my right shoulder. It began to turn very slowly down, down, down until it reached my heart.

"When it got there, the pain oddly subsided."

Bill, still standing at the lectern, glanced at the clock on the wall. It said 8:23 P.M.

"You know," he said to the class, "I don't feel well. You all go and take a ten-minute break while I just sit in a chair. If I don't feel any better after that, I'll let you go early tonight."

There was a shuffle in the room as backpacks were gathered and students headed out into the hall. One of them, however, a woman in her early thirties, came up to the lectern. Her face registered concern.

"Mr. Rot, I think you're sicker than you think you are. We've watched a big change in your countenance and color over the last few minutes. I'm going to send some guys to get the paramedics, and here's what I need you to do for me." With that, she started giving orders.

"Take off your suit coat, please." Bill obeyed. She moved the lectern table aside and spread the coat on the floor. "Now lie down here so we can get some blood flowing back to your face."

Bill at that moment had no way of knowing she had been a trainer at a women's fitness center and had been taught to read the signs of physical distress. But he went along with her guidance as she sat down on the floor beside him.

"I'm going to ask you questions, and you give me one-word answers, okay? Nothing longer than that. How many children do you have?"

"Four," Bill correctly answered.

"What is your wife's name?"

"Marilee."

Paramedics came dashing in almost immediately, because the college hires them to be on duty whenever classes are in session. They had minimal equipment though.

The questions continued. "Is your oldest grandchild a boy or a girl?"

"Girl."

Bill still felt no pain, but neither did he want to stand up and resume teaching. Soon the EMT truck arrived, and he was loaded onto a stretcher. Phone calls went out to Bill's wife and their son, who would meet them at Northwest Hospital in nearby Arlington Heights. Bill also heard the paramedics calling ahead to say, "We think we have a man with a heart problem, although there are no chest pains. So we don't really know what we're dealing with."

The ER doctor ran a few tests, scratched his head, and then made a wild guess as to a diagnosis: an upper thoracic aneurysm. In fact, he was exactly right. This is not a heart attack, where the channel gets clogged. Instead, the upper aorta *splits,* pumping blood into all the wrong places: the chest cavity, for one. In Bill's case, some of the blood also began to backflow toward the heart again, which created a pressure that ripped his aortic valve.

Medical history shows that the vast majority of people to whom this happens bleed to death within minutes. At the very least they suffer major brain damage for lack of adequate blood supply to the head. So for the student to have immediately gotten her teacher horizontal on the floor was a brilliant move.

A heart surgery team was quickly contacted, and Bill was rushed thirty minutes across the northern suburbs to their facility, Saint Francis Hospital in Evanston. Amazingly, he was still conscious. The attention of the God he had loved and served for decades was unusually present, he sensed. "On the ride, I was softly singing one of my favorite worship songs, 'I Love You, Lord,'" he remembers.

"Are you trying to tell us something?" the ambulance crew asked.

"No, I'm just being thankful to God."

They shrugged as if he were hallucinating.

During that drive, the Lord seemed to say something additional to Bill's spirit. "I want you to pray with the doctor before surgery."

Oh, I couldn't, he thought. *They wouldn't let me.*

But once he arrived in the bright lights of the Evanston hospital and was being prepped for surgery, he decided it wouldn't hurt to try. After the anesthesiologist had introduced herself and explained the upcoming procedure, Bill asked to meet the surgeon, a big man named Dr. Murphy.

The two men talked briefly about what would take place. Then Bill said, "I have a request. If it won't offend anybody, I'd like to pray with you all."

The surgeon looked down with a blank stare. Then he announced in his booming voice, "Hey, everyone, Bill wants to have a prayer before we start. Okay with you?" No one commented. Turning back to Bill, he ordered, "Well, go ahead and do it!"

"O God, give the doctors wisdom on what needs to be done. May you be glorified through this, and whatever happens, I will be content with it." Bill's peaceful attitude was noticeable.

The surgery was due to last all night. Dr. Murphy was very straightforward with Marilee and the children. "We're going to have to freeze his body for about ninety minutes in order to make the main repair by opening up his aorta, putting a Dacron liner inside, then stitching it closed again. To be honest with you, we seldom manage to save anybody through this surgery. But if I'm still working after seven hours, you'll know we're having very good luck. If you see me sooner, you'll immediately know we failed."

Talk about a trial, a testing.

The surgery began about a quarter after one in the morning. When the sun came up the next morning, Dr. Murphy still had not appeared in the family waiting room.

Shortly after eight o'clock, the good news was heard that Bill was still alive. The aorta was whole again, although there had not been enough time to replace the aortic valve. That condition could wait for later attention.

The anesthesiologist said to Marilee with a sense of wonder, "Your husband prayed with us last night before we started. I think that's the first time that's ever happened in our careers. And I want you to know something: I've never before been in a surgery where everything went perfectly. That was a real experience for all of us."

BACK TO WORK

The recovery for Bill Rot was long and tough, of course. He spent eleven days in intensive care. The family was summoned four different times to come for "the end." But it never occurred.

After three and a half weeks, he got out of the hospital. He wasn't back at the Penney store for three months. It was six months before he could work a full schedule.

But when he returned, Bill was noticeably different. His employees could see it. "This taught me to be more compassionate," he says. "I'd always been a typical Type A personality. This trauma made me dwell on the truly important things in life: my walk with Christ, my wife, my children, and their families. These are the things that are really important.

"At the store, I zeroed in much more on my employees as people, not as commodities. From that time forward, I built much stronger relationships. When opportunities came along to share Christ, I took them. One saleswoman whom I led to Christ was suffering with cancer. She eventually died after a four-year struggle. Her priest openly admitted he didn't quite know what to say at her funeral, and so her husband asked me to speak.

"It was a highlight of my career as a JCPenney manager."

Bill's life today is more fulfilled and more fruitful than ever. He retired from the company awhile back and quickly got busy volunteering with the Willow Creek Association, a collection of churches eager to reach spiritual seekers (an outgrowth of the well-known Willow Creek Community Church in South Barrington, Illinois, one of America's largest). "A friend invited me to help organize the resource table at seminars for church leaders. To me, of course, this was just another form of retailing! Only now I'd be selling books and tapes and CDs instead of sweaters and socks.

"I organized a whole system for setup at the various venues around the country: display schemes, cash management, knockdown when the event is over—the whole package." In the first year he went on the road eight or so times. Then soon came a simulcast summit conference for leaders involving fifty-one sites on the same weekend.

He did so well that recently he was asked to be Willow Creek Association's event manager for all off-site conferences—still as a volunteer.

"I've been given additional years to my life," he says, looking back on the night in 1992 when he almost bled to death. "I personally believe God spared me for a reason. I have a real vision for this work. And I believe the Lord made me a better man to get ready for it."

GRADE AAA

This kind of second life is an example of the "good and perfect" gifts that James 1:17 mentions, coming from our unchanging, immutable God. No gift to us is the result of a bad day. There's no such thing on his calendar.

Aren't you glad God doesn't play games with us at gift-giving time? He doesn't arrange his testing to jerk us around. Instead, he has a clear goal in mind—and it's all for the good.

In the midst of a test, we may struggle to see the point. But time is a great healer. The meaning of our darkest days comes through two years, five years, or even ten years down the road. Only then can we explain it to others.

We begin at last to see the point of verse 18: "He chose to give us birth through the word of truth, that we might be a kind of firstfruits of all he created."

Long term, what God has in mind is for us to be his finest creations. He wants us to be "a kind of firstfruits." That's an agrarian term that most of us city dwellers find unfamiliar. It's farm talk. The background is this: The Israelites were instructed in the Old Testament to bring God the first-fruits of their crops as a celebration, an expression of thankfulness that the upcoming harvest would be bountiful. This meant they would stay alive for another year, because it would provide the family with a source of personal food as well as a portion that could be sold or bartered for other supplies.

The emphasis was not so much on the very first produce to appear as it was on the *finest* fruit. You didn't try to slough off by giving God the leftovers, the half-rotten fruit. Instead, you presented him with the first and best.

This verse in James says that because of our coming through suffering, we can be the very finest specimens of humanity that God could produce. We are meant to be the highest quality of all his creation. Yes, you and me!

What makes us Grade AAA? The pain of testing.

If we understand this as Christians, we will realize God's true purposes in our pain. We will also see that we have a role to play in helping each other through the refinement. Christians should not be those you *avoid* when you're in pain. They should be those you *run to*.

The unchanging, unvarying God knows what he is doing. Our part is to keep from bailing out of the program early. If we hang in there, we will emerge on the other side more valuable than ever.

- Describe Bill Rot's Second Wind experience in two or three sentences. Do you identify with this story?

_____

_____

_____

_____

- What synonyms come to mind when you see these words?
Trials

_____

_____

Testings

_____

_____

Temptations

_____

_____

- Let's look closer at how Scripture deals with these terms. Write a definition of each of the following words found in James 1. Begin by looking at the word itself and the words that surround it. Then feel free to consult a reliable Bible dictionary or encyclopedia.

Word   _Definition_

Joy

Trial

Testing

Faith

Word	_Definition_
Perseverance	
Finish	
Mature	
Complete	
Lacking anything	
Tempted	
Evil	
Enticed	
Desire	
Sin	
Death	
Does not change	
No variation	
Good	
Perfect	
Firstfruits	

- Are you currently experiencing some painful and difficult times? How can these scriptures be an encouragement to you?

  _____

  _____

  _____

  _____

  _____

  _____

- Based on what you've learned, write a brief letter to someone you know who is in pain. Offer them the explanations from Scripture along with your own personal hope and encouragement. You can decide whether to actually mail the letter or not, but the exercise of putting thoughts on paper will be helpful to you.

• What is the most important truth you gleaned from this chapter?

_____

_____

_____

_____

• Based on what you read in this chapter, how can *you* get a Second Wind?

_____

_____

_____

_____

_____

On Pain and Its Purposes

E. Stanley Jones (1884–1973)

A Methodist missionary to India during the colonial period, Jones learned a great deal from the distressed environment in which he lived. His prolific writing and speaking brought God's truth in fresh ways to audiences both Eastern and Western.

In 1930 he founded his first "ashram," a place for spiritual retreat that fit the Indian tradition but led many to consider the person of Christ. No doubt the richness of his devotional writing sprang in part from the times he spent there in reflection before God.

E. Stanley Jones wrote twenty-nine books in all, the best known of which is The Christ of the Indian Road *(1925). The following excerpt is taken from his classic devotional,* Abundant Living *(1942).*

Christianity survived the worst thing that could happen to it, namely, the death of its Founder, and turned that worst thing…into the best thing that could happen to the world. It redeemed the world through a catastrophe. A faith that can do that has survival value, and will outlast all the shallow-rooted, surface philosophies of life. Nothing less than that kind of a philosophy of life can stand up to life.

We can see why God allows pain—it is His preventive grace. Had there been no pain in the world, we should not have survived as a race. For instance, were there no pain attached to disease, we should probably allow disease to eat on—it doesn't hurt; so why bother? But pain stabs us broad awake and says: "Look out—there is something wrong here; attend to it." Pain is God's red flag run up to warn of underlying lurking danger. We can then thank God for pain.

But this we cannot do unless we can do something with pain other than bearing it stoically. Unless pain is working out to some end, it breaks us by its meaninglessness. That is why the prophet saw that "pagans waste their pains." (Jeremiah 51:58, Moffatt.) Those who live without the God-reference—the pagans—don't know what to do with pain; they waste it. Their pains end in mere dull, fruitless, meaningless suffering. It gets them nowhere. So much of the world's suffering is wasted. During 1914–18 [World War I] we suffered dreadfully, and yet we wasted that world pain. The best that we could do with it was to coin it into the Versailles Treaty; and now we are back again, compelled to go through the whole miserable business once more. We may do the same thing with this present world pain unless we can transmute it into a determined purpose to make a new world out of it, so that war may never happen again. Only where we see redemption in pain can we have any release while in it—purposeless pain is paralyzing.

...Paul speaks of "the pain God is allowed to guide" (II Corinthians 7:10, Moffatt)—there can be a God-guided pain. Pain can be taken up into the purposes of God and transformed into finer character, greater tenderness, and more general usefulness. It can be made into the pains of childbirth—it can bring forth new life.

Take one of the most difficult pains to bear—the frustration of one's life plans. This often throws confusion into everything, for everything had been geared into those life plans. How did Jesus meet such a situation? A small incident reveals His secret.

When Jesus healed the demoniac, the people came and saw the man, seated, "clothed, and in his right mind: and they were afraid." Afraid of sanity! They begged Jesus "to depart out of their coasts." His presence had cost them too much. He thought men were worth more than swine. Anyone who thinks that is dangerous! It is disconcerting—and to some, discouraging—to find one's best endeavors blocked by ignorance and self-centered greed.

But was Jesus blocked?... No; He was not blocked, but diverted. His grace...simply turned in another direction.... He did some of the greatest things of His life as a result of that blocking.... He healed a paralytic, called Matthew, taught regarding conservatism, healed a woman with a hemorrhage, raised the dead, and so on and on. The frustration turned to fruitfulness. If He couldn't do this, He could do that.... He gained not only victory, but victory—plus!

Perhaps you find yourself in difficulties and frustrations because of your Christian stand. Then you will have to do as John did: "I...found myself in the island called Patmos, for adhering to God's word"—isolated because of conviction. But the verse continues: "On the Lord's day I found myself rapt in the Spirit, and I heard a loud voice...calling, 'Write your vision.'" (Revelation 1:9-11, Moffatt.) Isolated from men, he saw heaven opened and received the vision of the coming victory. Isolation became revelation.

Are your life plans broken up? Then you can, by God's grace, make new and better ones.

It is simply impossible, in reference to suffering, always to explain why. You cannot unravel the mystery of suffering and give a logical answer. But, while you cannot explain the Why, you can learn the How—the How of victory over it and through it and around it. There is no logical answer, but there is a life answer—you can use suffering. It is much better to give a vital answer than a verbal one. Cease worrying over the Why, and get to the How![1]

CRYING OUT FOR LOVE

—Dean—

Psychiatrists tell us that if we could crawl inside the brain of the most demented, disturbed, whacked-out mental case in the asylum, we would find that all his babblings make perfect sense—to him. The most severely afflicted psychopath or schizophrenic sincerely believes he is being logical. There really is a vicious brigade of Civil War artillerymen who have come back from the grave just to get him (or whatever the particular fantasy may be). The rest of us may roll our eyes and sigh, but the individual patient doesn't think he's crazy at all. He is functioning coherently according to his perception of reality.

The same holds true of less disturbed men and women who walk the shopping malls and maybe even sit at the next desk to us in the workplace. The way they spend their weekends, the relationships into which they plunge, the addicting substances they swallow and smoke and even inject into their veins, the freedom with which they abuse credit cards...we shake our heads in dismay. We can see exactly where they're going wrong. *How stupid,* we say to ourselves. *She's heading straight for a crash. Why can't she see the self-destructive nature of her behavior? What's the matter with her anyway?*

Meanwhile, these people keep operating according to what seems reasonable to them, what feels good at the moment, what meets their inner yearnings. They seem oblivious to the downward spiral of their actions.

CAUGHT IN THE ACT

To cite one example: The vast majority of good, churchgoing people feel nothing but disgust for people who have affairs. Faithfulness in marriage and celibacy outside of marriage are cardinal points of Christian ethics. This is no secret; everybody is fully informed, right? So stay out of beds where you don't belong, we declare with righteous affirmation.

That was certainly the view of the teachers and Pharisees who brought a certain woman to Jesus in John 8. "They made her stand before the group and said to Jesus, 'Teacher, this woman was caught in the act of adultery. In the Law Moses commanded us to stone such women. Now what do you say?'" (verses 3-5).

Because we generally don't like the Pharisees, we are prone to criticize their harshness in this account, their humiliation of the woman. Preachers have also noted over the years that while they nailed the woman, they apparently let her male partner pull his clothes back on and disappear without consequence, thus evidencing a double standard. The religious leaders were too busy making the woman look really vile, degenerate, and sinful.

Not that any of us would condone what she was caught doing, of course. But the Pharisees' public arraignment seems a little over the top.

Still, what about the woman herself? Who was she? What had led to this dreadful day?

Was she mistreated as a child perhaps? Did she have a history of promiscuity, or was this her first time? Was she known in the town to be "easy," or on the other hand, was everyone shocked at the steamy news?

Was she already married to someone? If so, was it an unhappy marriage?

Was she incredibly lonely? How did she meet this other guy? How long ago did they first begin to fall for each other? What did she see in him that attracted her? Would she say she truly loved him? Or was she pressured into this illicit relationship?

Why weren't they more careful with their liaisons? Who was the main risktaker? Who had the bright idea to get together this day, resulting in their getting caught at the worst possible moment?

Now what was going through her mind as she was pushed along the stony street and into the presence of the rabbi from Nazareth? Was she panicked? embarrassed? humiliated? Or was she brazen? cocky? insolent?

We don't know the answers to any of these questions. The text doesn't tell us. (This text, in fact, almost didn't make it into the New Testament at all. More than a few early church fathers felt the story was too risqué to include in Holy Scripture.)

It would be nice to have more facts about this woman, because we are sure she must have quite a story. John's account is too short for our curiosity.

And Jesus doesn't ask for background facts. (Of course, being the Son of God, he didn't need to. He already knew.) Instead he concentrated on making a point to the accusers. With his finger he wrote in the dust. (What did he write? Don't ask, because there's no clue to tell us. Any answer you've heard over the years is sheer speculation.)

Then, with one deft sentence about relative levels of fault, he sent the Pharisees packing. They stroked their beards with puzzlement as they walked away.

This allowed Jesus to turn his attention back to the most open-minded person on the scene, the woman herself. He "straightened up and asked her, 'Woman, where are they? Has no one condemned you?'

" 'No one, sir,' she said.

" 'Then neither do I condemn you,' Jesus declared. 'Go now and leave your life of sin' " (verses 10-11).

His outlook is totally aimed at the future, not the past. Yet he does not whitewash the past, as modern society is often too eager to do; he clearly labels it a "life of sin." He tells the truth about what she has been doing. But his main thrust is "Go now. Move ahead with your life on a whole different track than before."

He is not interested in condemnation for condemnation's sake. He knows there are certain times in life when it's best *not* to apply the prescribed penalty, even though it may be based on a justifiable law. Instead, in this case he focuses on personal change. He wants this woman to experience a Second Wind. He wants to set her free to live in righteousness and God's blessing. No more furtive trysts with married men. No more seeking for love in messy places. Instead, he calls her to the embrace of her heavenly Father, who created her in the first place and wants the very best for her future.

AMY'S STORY

When you're the fourth born in a family of five, it's hard to stake out your individuality. And when you're the only girl among four brothers, it's even harder to compete for attention.

Amy Robnik found a way, however. A very dubious way.

By junior high she decided that the Christianity she had grown up with wasn't everything it claimed to be. If it were, how come her parents didn't get along better? They took the family to church every Sunday morning and Wednesday night, but it didn't seem to help their marriage very much.

And another thing: How come her dad lost his job as a computer programmer and the only new ones he could find were out of town? That meant he left their northern Minnesota town of Esko early each Monday morning, and Amy wouldn't see him again until late Friday night—just when she was at the age of needing him most.

The energetic blonde began dating early. The first boyfriend was not a Christian, although she remembers him as a fairly moral person. Soon there were others, and by age sixteen she was seriously contemplating having sex. Why not? The idea of marriage was not all that attractive after seeing her parents' example. Hardly any of Amy's friends at school, either girls or guys, were still virgins.

"But at the same time, I remember feeling that God sort of said if I'd wait till marriage, he would bless me with a husband who was a virgin, and I'd have a happy future. That made me feel warm and peaceful inside, like, *Wow, that would be awesome, if I could only keep up my end of the bargain.*"

She did not, however. Amy's early sexual experiences made her feel somewhat obligated to the boyfriend, and when he said he was going to stay in nearby Duluth, Amy found herself torn. She wanted to get away from home and go to a distant college as soon as possible. Reluctantly she broke up with him.

Amy's self-destructive behavior increased. "As soon as I turned eighteen, I moved out of the house and into my best friend's house. Things really went downhill fast. I was drinking, and I was hurting. Friends tried to tell me, 'Amy, you have a problem. You're an alcoholic.' But I wouldn't listen."

The summer after high-school graduation, yet another dating relationship hit the rocks, and in a troubled frame of mind, Amy headed off to a Christian college in the Twin Cities. She was in no mood to benefit from its atmosphere, while she quickly exploited its freedoms. "I just went crazy. I stopped going to church now that no one was forcing me. I was drinking a lot already, and I found other kids who would join me.

"A lot of them would party with me on the weekends and then pretend they didn't know me in school because they wanted to be seen as 'angels.' I was so turned off. I'd expound about Christian hypocrites. I've always been the kind of person who's exactly what you see; I'm not going to try to fake you out."

By the end of the first year, Amy concluded that the Christian campus was not the place for her. Where else could she go and be her real self? How about far, far away from Minnesota? That fall found Amy in the Deep South, at Auburn University in Alabama. Here there was no need even to think about Christianity. Alcohol was abundant, and so were drugs. She quickly found a crowd that made her comfortable.

"The more I drank, the more I lost my values, and the more I slept around. I made more and more mistakes," she says today with sadness. "There were some close calls at times with drug dealers, but I always managed to escape."

She had enough natural talent to keep making good grades. This helped her rationalize: *I'm not an alcoholic. Alcoholics are bums. They don't make A's like I'm doing.*

Amy actively pursued friendships with African American students, who were more plentiful there than in Minnesota. It became another part of her self-differentiation. While many of these friends were avid partygoers, there was also a Christian girl named Annie who became a close soul mate. "We talked a lot. She showed me so much love. She knew everything I was doing, but she never condemned me or wrote me off. She would just ask me innocent questions, like 'Amy, have you prayed recently?'"

Her fast life continued in her junior year of college, and with the coming of her twenty-first birthday on November 4, she was now totally legal to enter any bar—although being underage had seldom stopped her up to this point. She looked forward to this day as her final emancipation.

At the same time, Amy had to admit that her reckless behavior was getting a little old. Nothing seemed to make her feel fulfilled. She was depressed, at times almost suicidal. She told Annie about her inner doubts and then blurted out as a last resort, "What if I went to church with you sometime?"

Annie smiled and said yes, of course. They arranged that on the following Sunday they would get up early and drive two hours south to Annie's home church near Ozark, Alabama, not far from the Florida Panhandle.

The Saturday night before, Amy went out drinking with some friends. Around one o'clock in the morning the thought hit her inebriated brain, *I really should go home now. I have to get up early in the morning to go to church!*

The alarm went off at six o'clock, and Amy reluctantly rolled out of bed. She lit a cigarette to try to jump-start her body. All too soon Annie and another friend were knocking on her door, smiling and ready to start the day's journey. Amy greeted them with a grunt, then crawled into the car and slept most of the way.

When she awakened at last, she found herself approaching a small, all-black holiness church in the country, with fields on every side. The sky was beautifully clear. "I looked up at the white steeple and thought, *Okay, here we go. Whatever...*

"Inside, I was the only white face in the building. And I was definitely the only person in jeans and a sweater! Every other woman in the place wore a Sunday dress and her hair in a bun, it seemed. The man teaching adult Sunday school wore a white suit.

"An hour later the worship service began. The music had all the soul you would expect in such a place. The preacher wore a long robe, and his sermon quickly fell into the classic singsong rhythm. I don't remember his text—only his manner: He was very loving. I was entranced.

"Somewhere in the middle of his sermon, he sort of interrupted himself and said, 'Somebody needs to come forward to this altar right now.' *Bam!* I was up and on my feet, hardly realizing I was moving."

Women of the congregation soon gathered around the scruffy college student, imploring God to move into her heart and wash it clean at last. Amy remembers the occasion almost in surreal terms. Time stood still. "I was calling out to the Lord, and people kept saying to me, 'Just receive, honey, just receive.'"

To let the service proceed to its natural conclusion, the deaconesses guided Amy to a side room to continue praying. She remembers at one point the sensation of a big white light.

And then the women, with all warmth and love, began to say, "If you really want the Lord to come live within you, there are some things you need to let go. Just confess them to God. Go ahead and repent."

Amy didn't have trouble thinking of things. First on the list was unforgiveness toward her mother. Then came her sexual life. Next was drinking. One by one, she spelled out her sins to God and agreed to give them up. The scene was emotional and tearful, but underneath there was genuine penitence too.

Hours flew by, and the morning turned into afternoon. The praying continued. At last everyone stood up for a round of fervent hugs. The minister's wife exhorted her, "Here's your keyword, Amy: *faith, faith, faith.* You're a new creation. You walk by faith now. You're not the same person you were when you got up this morning."

Then she followed with "Would you like to be baptized today? You really should." Amy nodded her head as she wiped away her tears.

The service had been dismissed, but the families of the women who had been praying with Amy were still around. In a few minutes, she entered the baptistery and was immersed as a sign of her new life in Christ.

"I remember how all the little black kids were fascinated with watching this white girl go down into the water and come back up again!" she says with a laugh. "But more than that, the baptism showed how my old self was dying and my new self was coming alive. I'm glad they insisted."

It was half past three in the afternoon when Amy finally came out of that little church into the sunshine. It had been an overwhelming day. As she crawled back into the car for the return trip to Auburn, she was a little confused on some doctrinal points, but she knew what had happened was real. Her memory flashed back to how drunk she had been just the night before, and she knew God had now filled her with his Spirit to empower her for overcoming those things. Otherwise, she was sure her turnaround would not last.

"When I walked back into my apartment that evening, there were my pajamas still lying on the bathroom floor from the morning shower. I stared at them. In an odd sort of way, they symbolized the old me, now discarded for something far better. I was a new person.

"I'd never thought I was good enough to be a Christian. Now I was cleansed, forgiven, and headed onto a new road altogether."

A LIFE REDEEMED

In the weeks and months that followed, Amy's life was not without struggle and even a relapse one night when a friend wanted to take her to a bar. But with the help of campus Bible studies, a nearby church, and her family's encouragement, she made steady progress.

One day on the phone, her mother said, "Amy, when you come home for Christmas, the pastor here wants you to share your testimony in church."

"*No way!*" she responded. "I will *not* do that. I can't possibly face those people after all the stuff they watched me do when I was in high school."

But after several more requests, Amy finally gave in. The day came. She stood in front of her girlhood church—and began crying. She could not say a word for several minutes. As she looked out at the congregation, there were tears all over the building.

Finally she began to speak. It turned out to be a powerful witness of the life-changing power of God.

Some of Amy's high school friends had come to hear her that morning. While some applauded her, others said, "You're in your religious phase now. You'll get over it."

But Amy has never gotten over it. More than nine years have passed since that day, and her walk with God remains solid. She finished her degree at Auburn and then continued at Christian Life College in the Chicago suburb of Mount Prospect, studying for a future in youth ministry. There she met a young man named Eric Joob with a similar desire to help urban young people. Their friendship deepened. Amy knew, of course, that sooner or later she would have to reveal the details of her past. She dreaded that day.

"Finally I got up the courage to tell him all of my history. I was so scared. But God had prepared his heart to hear it."

The amazing thing, she then learned, was that even though Eric had grown up in the city, been part of a gang, and had experimented with drinking and drugs—he was still a virgin. Says Amy: "The dream of my high school days long ago came true in spite of what I had done. It's like that verse in 2 Timothy 2:13—'If we are faithless, he will remain faithful, for he cannot disown himself.'"

Eric and Amy were married in 1998, and for three years Amy managed a teen drop-in center. She also has done some modeling and acting and competed in a triathlon. She is a living example of God's ability to forgive mistakes and breathe new life and health into any person crying out for wholeness.

The craziness of the past does not have to dictate the future. We can learn to think in new ways according to God's truth. He stands before us as he did with the woman centuries ago, looking us in the eye, and saying, "Go now." As we let his Holy Spirit propel us in a new direction, we find ourselves happier and more complete than we ever thought possible.

- "Crying out for love"—can you relate to those words? If so, describe your feelings in a paragraph or two. If not, why not? Do you know somebody who feels that way? How can you reach out to him or her?

  _____

  _____

  _____

  _____

  _____

  _____

- Does Amy Robnik's story of college rebellion remind you of any particular time in your life? How is your life similar to Amy's? How is it different?

  _____

  _____

  _____

  _____

  _____

- The account of the woman caught in adultery from John 8 is a familiar one to many of us. In order to personalize this passage and to add freshness to it, let's once again try *paraphrasing*. Rewrite John 8:1-11 in your own words. Try to go beyond the words in the text by digging deeply into the feelings and emotions that are symbolized by these words.

  _____

  _____

• At the end of this chapter it says: "The craziness of the past does not have to dictate the future. We can learn to think in new ways according to God's truth." Do you believe those words? Does God's forgiveness include *your* past? How does this topic relate to your own personal Second Wind?

_____

_____

_____

_____

_____

_____

• Spend a few minutes talking to your Father in prayer. Tell him how much you love him. Ask him to forgive you for the craziness of your past. Tell him about your hopes and dreams for the future as a result of your Second Wind. Thank him for his involvement in your life.

• What is the most important truth you gleaned from this chapter?

_____

_____

_____

_____

_____

_____

• Based on what you read in this chapter, how can *you* get a Second Wind?

_____

_____

_____

_____

_____

_____

On Coming Back to God's Favor

John Wesley (1703–91)

Founder of the Methodist movement, the untiring John Wesley preached tens of thousands of sermons not only in England's churches but even more often in the open air. Some historians credit the spiritual awakening he led with preventing a bloody upheaval like the French Revolution that raged just across the English Channel at the end of Wesley's era.

One of his messages, excerpted here, was based on Psalm 77:7-8, "Will the Lord reject forever? Will he never show his favor again? Has his unfailing love vanished forever? Has his promise failed for all time?"

It [may] be asked [of me], "Do any real apostates find mercy from God? Do any that have 'made shipwreck of faith and a good conscience,' recover what they have lost? Do you know, have you seen, any instance of persons who found redemption in the blood of Jesus, and afterwards fell away, and yet were restored,—'renewed again to repentance?'" Yea, verily; and not one, or an hundred only, but, I am persuaded, several thousands. In every place where the arm of the Lord has been revealed, and many sinners converted to God, there are several found who…"look unto him they have pierced, and mourn," refusing to be comforted. And, sooner or later, he surely lifts up the light of his countenance upon them; he strengthens the hands that hang down, and confirms the feeble knees; he teaches them again to say, "My soul doth magnify the Lord, and my spirit rejoiceth in God my Saviour." Innumerable are the instances of this kind, of those who had fallen, but now stand upright....

It is a common thing for those who are…sanctified, to believe they cannot fall; to suppose themselves "pillars in the temple of God, that shall go out no more." Nevertheless, we have seen some of the strongest of them, after a time, moved from their steadfastness. Sometimes suddenly, but oftener by slow degrees, they have yielded to temptation; and pride, or anger, or foolish desires have again sprung up in their hearts. Nay, sometimes they have utterly lost the life of God, and sin hath regained dominion over them.

Yet...several of these, after being thoroughly sensible of their fall, and deeply ashamed before God, have been again filled with his love, and not only perfected therein, but stablished, strengthened, and settled. They have received the blessing they had before with abundant increase.... They have, at once, recovered both a consciousness of his favour, and the experience of the pure love of God....

But let not any man infer from this longsuffering of God, that he hath given any one a license to sin. Neither let any dare to continue in sin, because of these extraordinary instances of divine mercy. This is the most desperate, the most irrational presumption, and leads to utter, irrecoverable destruction. In all my experience, I have not known one who fortified himself in sin by a presumption that God would save him at the last [moment], that was not miserably disappointed, and suffered to die in his sins. To turn the grace of God into an encouragement to sin is the sure way to the nethermost hell.

It is not for these desperate children of perdition that the preceding considerations are designed; but for those who feel "the remembrance of their sins is grievous unto them, the burden of them intolerable." We set before these an open door of hope: Let them go in and give thanks unto the Lord; let them know that "the Lord is gracious and merciful, long-suffering, and of great goodness." "Look how high the heavens are from the earth! so far will he set their sins from them." "He will not always be chiding; neither keepeth he his anger for ever." Only settle it in your heart, *I will give all for all,* and the offering shall be accepted. Give him all your heart! Let all that is within you continually cry out, "Thou art my God, and I will thank thee; thou art my God, and I will praise thee." "This God is my God for ever and ever! He shall be my guide even unto death."[1]

CHAPTER 10

WAIT A MINUTE

—Bill—

Whenever you read a book such as this one, with its offer of hope that life could be better than it is today, the natural response is to say, "Yes! I really want that. Bring it on. Oh, it would be so good to experience a Second Wind in my miserable situation."

We want God to intervene dramatically, and the sooner the better.

Of course, the matter is not entirely in our control, is it? If we could kick off our own renaissance all by ourselves, we would have done it a long time ago. In fact, some of us have tried. But there's a divine element here, and it moves according to a divine schedule.

The disciples of Jesus found that out in the days following their leader's return to heaven. They had watched him die on the cross, rise from the dead, and then ascend. They had ridden waves of emotion and energy—up and down and back up again—and now what? Jesus was gone. He wasn't stepping into view from around the corner as he had done for the past forty days. He was truly gone to another world this time. And they were left with fear, uncertainty, and anxiousness. They felt very alone.

The first day after the Ascension passed. The second. The third. Jesus had promised them that the Holy Spirit would come upon them—whatever that was supposed to mean. They kept waiting through the fourth day. The fifth. The sixth.

A whole week passed. What was going on all this time?

Nothing much. Just waiting. That is what Jesus had told them to do. "Do not leave Jerusalem, but wait for the gift my Father promised, which you have heard me speak about" (Acts 1:4).

Wait. A lot of us don't particularly like that word. We don't like it flashing yellow at us at a crosswalk. We don't like it when our computer is booting up, and that maddening little hourglass on the screen keeps doing its thing. We don't like it when the freeway turns into a parking lot. We even get impatient with the microwave.

I hate to wait! Whatever I want, I want it now. I want to be spiritually mature—right now! I want perfect relationships without any time and work—right now!

Vincent de Paul back in the 1600s said, "Those who are in a hurry delay the things of God." Ouch. More recently I heard this wise maxim: "The only thing harder than waiting on God is wishing we had." We've all done that a few times in our lives: jumped the gun to make our own solution instead of waiting for God's far better one.

What were the disciples thinking about during those quiet days? I don't know for sure, but it wouldn't surprise me that they were focusing on Jesus, the one who had just left them. At the moment of ascension, the Bible says, "they were looking intently" (verse 10) as he rose up. He was in the center of their vision. I can well imagine that they locked in on him for the duration.

We do know that as they waited, the atmosphere was such that Luke could record, "They all joined together" (verse 14). They were unified. Anyone who thought that the Holy Spirit would come in isolation was mistaken.

People today sometimes say, "I don't need all these stupid Christians anymore. I can do it my own way." The foibles and idiosyncrasies of fellow believers have caused so much frustration that they've pulled away.

The disciples stayed "joined together," because they were engaged in a common pursuit. In their unity, they were "constantly in prayer" (verse 14). They were pouring out their hearts to the Lord to come and fill them.

The eighth day passed. The ninth. The tenth day arrived, the Jewish feast called Pentecost, because it was fifty days after Passover. And as they were still focused and unified, "all together in one place" (Acts 2:1), the Holy Wind came upon them in a very big way.

Did you know that the Greek word for *spirit* is *pneuma,* which can also be translated "wind" or "breath"? It's the root from which we get such English terms as *pneumatic,* as in a drill that runs on air pressure. If you have *pneumonia,* it means your wind isn't moving very well. The Holy Pneuma is God's mighty wind blowing into our stale lives.

When Jesus spoke to Nicodemus in John 3, he said, "The wind *[pneuma]* blows wherever it pleases. You hear its sound, but you cannot tell where it comes from or where it is going. So it is with everyone born of the Spirit *[Pneuma]*" (verse 8).

When Paul stood before the intelligentsia of Athens, he spoke about a God who "gives everyone life and breath *[pnoe,* a derivative of *pneuma]* and everything else" (Acts 17:25).

On this particular day in Jerusalem, the invasion of the Holy Spirit was accompanied by something audible. They could actually hear "a sound like the blowing of a violent wind" (Acts 2:2). The Greek word here, as in Acts 17, is *pnoe.* This tornado was more than a coincidence. The Holy Pneuma literally *blew* into their lives.

At the same time, there was something that could be seen—"tongues of fire that separated and came to rest on each of them" (verse 3). God's empowering was becoming a multimedia event. Sound, sight, feel—all were involved.

Finally this divine incursion affected the believers' speech (verse 4). Instead of mumbling around and wasting words, they were suddenly able to make an impact with what they said. They gave voice to "the wonders of God," according to those who crowded around to listen (verse 11).

All of this added up to what the Bible calls being "filled with the Holy Spirit" (verse 4). These believers received *power,* according to Acts 1:8. As you may know, the Greek word here is *dunamis,* from which we get the word *dynamite.* Not just the power of a couple of AA batteries in your travel clock. Instead, a major explosion.

Was it worth the ten days' wait? You bet!

The same reenergizing power is available to you and me. It wasn't just a flukish phenomenon for that particular group. As the apostle Peter explained to the crowd that day at the end of his message, "The promise is for you and your children and for all who are far off—for all whom the Lord our God will call" (Acts 2:39).

God can energize you in a way you haven't experienced before. As a result, you can smash through the wall in your life. But he will do it in his time, not yours.

Young Man in a Hurry

My friend Jeff Pries was born and bred to be a baseball pitching ace. His dad worked in the front office of the Oakland A's when Jeff was little and then became assistant general manager of the Baltimore Orioles. These were the glory years, when the Orioles went to the World Series three times in a row (1969–71). The kid almost grew up with a glove on his hand and a strike zone on the front wall of his brain.

Up through the Little League levels he rose, until when he reached Corona del Mar High School in the late 1970s (not far from where I live today), he was fearsome on the mound. He made batters look absolutely foolish. He lost not a single game his entire high school career; he was 20–0. That got him the Player of the Year award from the CIF (California Interscholastic Federation). His dad and mom could not have been prouder.

"Baseball was my identity," Jeff remembers. "It defined who I was. Yes, I had become a Christian during my sophomore year after feeling a vague sense that there must be something more to life. But it wasn't front-burner for me. Throwing hard sliders and wicked curve balls was what I was really all about."

For college he moved up the freeway to UCLA, one of the prime collegiate baseball programs in the nation. Again he was impressive. "I majored in baseball and played sociology," he says today with a grin.

He began noticing a little arm trouble once in a while but nothing serious. When the New York Yankees scouted and then drafted him after his junior year as their number-one pick in 1984, he wrote off the last year of college to turn pro. The future looked marvelous.

Up through the ranks he came over the next year or two, from the A leagues to AA and on to the Yankees' AAA farm team in Columbus, Ohio. The only trouble was, the arm began to hurt more, and Jeff wasn't quite as overpowering on the mound. The call to head for Yankee Stadium didn't come.

It was disappointing to get sent back down to the AA team in Albany, New York…and then even back to the A-level club in Fort Lauderdale, Florida. Buck Showalter, then on his way up as a young manager, called Jeff into his office one day and laid into him. "Hey, kid, what's the matter?" he demanded. "This organization has spent a bunch of money and time on you. The bosses are expecting a lot. How come you're not coming through for us?"

Jeff could only weakly reply, "I don't know, man…my arm hurts."

The Yankees lost patience and traded Jeff to the Chicago White Sox, who put him in their Sarasota, Florida, instruction league. Soon the doctors discovered a torn rotator cuff and a torn labrum. Surgery was done, followed by a long period of rehabilitation.

"I worked like crazy," Jeff says. "I figured if I'd do everything right, God would heal my arm." He even gave time to organize a baseball chapel for the club.

But the old form never returned. Finally in 1991, weary of the never-ending pain, he cleaned out his locker for the last time. Telling his dad was one of the hardest things Jeff had ever done.

NOW WHAT?

Back home in California, the twenty-eight-year-old bounced from one job to another, but soon he decided to finish school. He headed for the Northwest to enroll at Seattle Pacific University, a Christian college. But he didn't live on campus or get involved in the spiritual life of the school; he holed up in his apartment with his dog. "I had no friends, no family nearby. I basically ran away from life. I started drinking. It was all downhill from there."

Without baseball, who was Jeff Pries anyway?

A year went by. One night after sitting at a bar for hours, he finally stepped outside, lost consciousness, and landed in the gutter. He only half noticed when somebody came along and mugged him, relieving him of his remaining money.

Then a kinder soul—Jeff still doesn't know who—picked him up, figured out his address, pushed him into a cab, and told the driver to take him home. As the sun was coming up the next morning, Jeff finally regained consciousness to find himself lying on his own front porch.

"That did it. I said to myself, *You have to change, pal.* I knew I needed to run back to God and to my family."

He rented a U-Haul, packed up his belongings, and headed back down Interstate 5 toward Southern California. He was embarrassed, broken, devastated. The one-time professional ballplayer got a menial job in a restaurant to pay his bills. And he started going to Lake Hills Church in Lake Forest.

A few months later the church asked if Jeff would like to be an intern with their high school ministry. He said yes. He began working with high school kids, trying to steer them toward more durable foundations in life.

This went on for several years, during which he met Barbara, who eventually became his wife. In 1997 Mariners Church in Newport Beach invited him to become a full-time high school pastor.

"I'd always wanted to make something of my life," Jeff says. "They gave me a second chance to be significant in a different way than baseball.

"I wasn't wild about the pastoral 'image,' because I thought it was kind of soft. But in ministering to young people, I found my niche. I could still be real, even edgy at times.

"When you're a pitcher, you learn to look unfazed, regardless of what happens. You may have just given up a three-run homer, but you never let it show. You step up there and throw the ball all the harder. This trait serves me well in youth ministry! I may blow something, but the kids never catch a hint."

Today Jeff also works with young couples and small groups in the church. He occasionally speaks from the pulpit on a Sunday, although that's not his aspiration for the future. He and Barbara are the proud parents of two boys and two girls.

"God has given me as much as baseball ever could," he says. "Not as much money, to be sure—but tons of other things that I deeply cherish. In due time I came around to get in sync with his plan for me."

THE LONG VIEW

Waiting for the Second Wind in life is a complex thing we may never fully understand. In Jeff's case, he clearly postponed the renewal by the way he was living. But in the end, God came through regardless.

What do you do while you're waiting? I notice a number of good directives in Psalm 37.

The very first verse says, "Do not fret because of evil men." Don't let your emotions get tangled up with worry. It will only paralyze you as you wait.

The next phrase warns against being "envious of those who do wrong." In other words, don't get your head into thinking about those who are better off and got there by questionable means. So what? The comparison game is always a dead end.

Instead, says verse 3, "Trust in the LORD and do good." We're back to the concept of focusing on Jesus, as the disciples did. When we put our hopes entirely on him, we're not distracted with other options that are likely to fail.

In fact, we can even get our emotions into the act. "Delight yourself in the LORD," says verse 4, "and he will give you the desires of your heart." He makes us happy! It's okay.

All of this makes it more conducive for us to place our whole weight on God and his future for us. That is what verse 5 means when it says, "Commit your way to the LORD; trust in him and he will do this."

When?

"Be still before the LORD and wait patiently for him" (verse 7). The timing is not to be our issue. We will never be able to predict what God has in mind or when he intends to unfold it. Our job is simply to be ready, available, and cooperative. A reprise of the same theme shows up in verse

34. "Wait for the LORD and keep his way. He will exalt you to inherit the land; when the wicked are cut off, you will see it."

I have kept a personal journal for more than two decades. Not long ago I packed up all the notebooks I had filled, went off to a quiet place, and read them from start to finish. I had a ringside seat to observe my own life.

One of the key themes that emerged from that reading was this: *God is the only one who won't disappoint.* Humans will. The finest of humans. The best of friends. The closest of family. We can't help it. It's in our nature. People fail; God doesn't.

He knows when we need some additional time, even if we think otherwise. And eventually the desires of our heart come true.

PERSONAL JOURNAL

- After reading the story of Jeff Pries, can you assemble your thoughts
  and reflections into two or three summary sentences?

  _____

  _____

  _____

  _____

- Are there parts of Jeff's story with which you identify? Which parts?
  Are some parts of his story not exactly like your life, but they could
  symbolize certain aspects? If so, which parts?

  _____

  _____

  _____

  _____

  _____

- Reread Acts 1 and 2 with the specific purpose of looking for parts of
  the account that show *waiting*. Jot down your thoughts in the chart
  that follows. Then go back to Psalm 37 and do the same thing.

  <u>Reference</u>   <u>Thoughts on Waiting</u>

  Acts 1

Reference   _Thoughts on Waiting_

Acts 2

Psalm 37

• Are *you* waiting for the Second Wind in your life? Why do you think
  God is making you wait? What lessons are you learning? How are
  you different because of the wait?

  _____

  _____

  _____

  _____

  _____

  _____

• Take a few minutes to reread Psalm 37:34. It is such a strong verse
  on waiting that you may want to commit it to memory. Reflect on
  its message regularly this week.

• What is the most important truth you gleaned from this chapter?

  _____

  _____

  _____

_____

_____

_____

- Based on what you read in this chapter, how can *you* get a Second Wind?

_____

_____

_____

_____

_____

_____

ON GRACE

Charles H. Spurgeon (1834–92)

During more than three decades in the pulpit of London's Metropolitan Taber-
nacle, Spurgeon spoke often and passionately about the grace of God—not only
for the seeker but for the struggling Christian as well. That may have had some-
thing to do with the fact that the congregation grew to six thousand (in an era
without electric sound amplification!), and sales of his printed sermons hit
twenty-five thousand copies a week.

Here are some of his best gems on the subject:

Observe the rain which drops from heaven. It falls on the desert as well as
on the fertile field. It drops on the rock that will refuse its fertilizing mois-
ture as well as on the soil that opens its gaping mouth to drink it in with
gratitude. It falls on the streets of the city, where it is not required, and where
men will even curse it for coming, and it falls not more freely where the
sweet flowers have been panting for it and the withering leaves have been
rustling forth their prayers. Such is the grace of God. It does not visit us
because we ask for it, much less because we deserve it, but as God wills it.

I sometimes think if men did but understand grace they would be sure to
accept the Lord Jesus. I heard of a minister in Edinburgh who went to visit
one of his poor people. He heard that she was in deep poverty, and therefore he went to take her help. When he came to her house, he could not
make anybody hear, though he knocked loud and long. Seeing her

sometime after, he said, "Janet, I knocked at your door with help for you, but you did not hear me."

"What time did you come, sir?" said she.

"It was about 12 o'clock."

"Oh," she said, "I did hear you, but I thought it was the man calling for the rent."

Just so. Men do hear the calls of Christ, but they are willfully deaf, because they think he wants them to do something. But he does not want anything of you; he wants you to receive what he has already done. He comes laden with mercy, with his hands full of blessing, and he knocks at your door. You have only to open it and he will enter in.

―――――――

If sin will be the ruin of men—and surely it will—yet our Lord Jesus Christ knows how to take the ruined sinners and build them up to be temples for his indwelling. Christ will take the very castaways of the devil and use them for himself. He delights to stoop over the [garbage dump] and pick up a broken vessel that is thrown away, and make it into a vessel fit for the Master's use.

―――――――

I do not wonder that John Bradford [sixteenth-century preacher whom Mary Tudor—"Bloody Mary"—eventually burned at the stake] said, as he saw men taken to be hanged at Tyburn, "There goes John Bradford, but for the grace of God." There is powder enough in all our hearts to blow our character to pieces if God does not keep the devil's sparks away, or quench them in a mighty stream of grace before they can do us mischief.

———•———

Sin comes up like Noah's flood, but grace rides over the tops of the mountains like the ark. Sin, like Sennacherib [Assyrian general who attacked Hezekiah's Jerusalem], pours forth its troops to swallow up the land; grace, like the angel of the Lord, goes through the camp of Sennacherib and lays sin dead.

———•———

Man by nature is as a wild horse dashing to the precipice. If he be restrained in his course and turned away from danger, it is because he has a mighty Rider, and one that knows how to pull the bit and guide him as he pleases. And though he kick and plunge and long to turn away, his Rider can pull him up on his very haunches, turn him around, and make him go as he wills. In this matter it is true that all the bringing home of the gospel to the soul of man is of God.

———•———

Difficulty is not a word to be found in the dictionary of heaven. Nothing can be impossible with God. The swearing reprobate, whose mouth is blackened with profanity, whose heart is a very hell, and his life like the reeking flames of the bottomless pit—such a man, if the Lord but looks on him and makes bare his arm of irresistible grace, shall yet praise God and bless his name and live to his honor. Do not limit the Holy One of Israel.

CHAPTER 11

BEYOND OUR WILDEST DREAMS

—Dean—

Many of the profiles in this book have shown people who were stuck or derailed in life and finally got back to equilibrium. They had put themselves (or had been plunged by others) into a deep pit. They had sunk into a mess. And the Holy Spirit of God lifted them up to level ground again, for which they are immensely grateful.

But sometimes God does even more than that. He gets totally carried away. He starts to intervene in a person's life, and he winds up doing *"exceeding abundantly above* all that we ask or think" (Ephesians 3:20, KJV, emphasis added). He gives us a future beyond our wildest dreams.

Such was the case with an elderly couple in Scripture named Zechariah and Elizabeth. The gospel of Luke starts off telling how they lived in a tiny burg at the edge of the desert, far from anywhere. Not much to do besides watch the tumbleweeds roll by. They had already joined AARP. Their days passed quietly, Zechariah performing the clerical duties of a Jewish priest week after week. Once in a great while, the schedule on the wall would call him to trek off to the big city for a week of temple duty. Otherwise, it was a dull existence for the white-haired man and his wife.

They were models of goodness, salt of the earth, completely upright—the kind of people you'd ask to watch your kids for the weekend. But they silently bore a personal sadness—the lack of children of their own. After so many years had passed, there was nothing more to say about the subject. The house had never bounced with the noise of a child or grandchild and never would. Menopause had come, and they were resigned to their fate.

Then, on one of Zechariah's trips to the city, something absolutely crazy happened. An angel barged into his liturgical performance talking nonsense. Something about Zechariah and Elizabeth having a baby!

Yeah, sure.

In fact, the angel said this would be a very special son who would play a key role in the revival of the nation. "Many of the people of Israel will he bring back to the Lord their God. And he will go on before the Lord, in the spirit and power of Elijah, to turn the hearts of the parents to their children and the disobedient to the wisdom of the righteous—to make ready a people prepared for the Lord" (Luke 1:16-17).

Zechariah was understandably skeptical.

What this story illustrates is that God sometimes has some very strange ideas about our potential. He sees things we don't see at all. I mean, if you wanted someone to produce a leader who would rock a nation, calling it to its knees in preparation for the Messiah, would you select this pair of parents? They lived far from the cultural advantages of Jerusalem. They could provide no after-school enrichment classes or tutoring. No trips to the museum or the symphony. And they obviously would have no other siblings in the home for their son to grow up with, to socialize with, to adjust to. He would be an only child.

Plus, could a woman of Elizabeth's age even get through a pregnancy safely? We can well imagine what a modern ob-gyn would have said at the first appointment: "Now, Elizabeth, you need to understand the high risks involved here. A fair number of things could go wrong. Perhaps you should think about 'alternatives.' If you would like to consider 'termination,' I can be of assistance."

Thank God no such "wisdom" was voiced two thousand years ago. The apostle Paul wrote:

Brothers and sisters, think of what you were when you were called. Not many of you were wise by human standards; not many were influential; not many were of noble birth. But God chose the foolish things of the world to shame the wise; God chose the weak things of the world to shame the strong. He chose the lowly things of this world and the despised things—and the things that are not—to nullify the things that are, so that no one may boast before him. (1 Corinthians 1:26-29)

It takes our breath away to realize that God sees more in us than we see in ourselves! We think we are stuck in life; opportunity has passed us by; we must now just play out the string. And God says, "No! I have an idea."

BE CAREFUL ABOUT BELITTLING GOD'S IDEAS

The elderly priest protested, "How can I be sure of this? I am an old man and my wife is well along in years" (Luke 1:18).

Big mistake, Zechariah. Didn't your mother ever teach you that if you can't say something good about a situation, don't say anything? Zechariah would have been better off just nodding in silence—because that's exactly what he got to do for the next nine months. The angel shot back, "I am Gabriel. I stand in the presence of God, and I have been sent to speak to you and to tell you this good news. And now you will be silent and not able to speak until the day this happens, because you did not believe my words, which will come true at their appointed time" (verses 19-20).

That may seem harsh, and God doesn't always crack down this hard on unbelief. But sometimes, yes.

The contrast of the two utterances is stark. One person says, "I am an old man," and the other replies, "Yes, but so what? I am Gabriel."

To every person who says, "Lord, I'm nobody special," God replies, "I am the Lord who made you in the first place."

To everyone who complains, "I never got to finish college," he replies, "I am the omniscient one, the source of all knowledge."

To everyone who says, "I can't make ends meet this month, and I don't know what to do," he answers, "I am Jehovah-jireh, the God who supplies."

To every mom who cries, "I'm a single parent, and these kids are driving me nuts," he says, "I am a father to the fatherless."

Zechariah came out of the temple at last—and couldn't explain a thing! He was expected at this point to pronounce upon the waiting crowd the Aaronic blessing of Numbers 6: "The LORD bless you and keep you..." (verses 24-26). Instead, all he could do was wave his arms and point, like a third-base coach in the ninth inning with the bases loaded. People certainly went home with lots to talk about that day.

I wonder what it was like the next day when Zechariah arrived back in the desert village to break the news to his wife. They must have had quite a time—him writing on a tablet and gesturing, Elizabeth reading his scribbles and then gasping. What a shock. Her only recorded response comes a few months later when she has realized that in fact she's pregnant, and she comments with gratitude, "The Lord has done this for me. In these days he has shown his favor and taken away my disgrace among the people" (Luke 1:25).

In time, the baby arrives safe and sound. Zechariah's initial hesitation had not spoiled God's plan after all. In fact, by this time, the father is more than willing to get with the program, even if it means going against family tradition. Everybody expects him to name his son Zechariah. No, he writes on the tablet, "His name is John." And with that, his speech instantaneously returns.

You've heard of Murphy's Law. Well, there's also something called Cornford's Law, which goes like this:

Nothing is ever done until everyone is convinced that it ought to be done and has been convinced for so long that it is now time to do something else.

How true!
Cornford's Law has a corollary that says:

Nothing should ever be done for the first time.

Zechariah and Elizabeth were willing to do something for the first time. They were on board with God's big idea whether Aunt Mabel approved or not. They knew that to cooperate with God sometimes means going against tradition.

In fact, the last years of this couple's life were the best years of all: They got to raise a son! Their house came alive with joy and fun and blessing. Their fondest dreams became reality. What God wanted to do in their lives became sheer pleasure.

ALL OPTIONS OPEN

—Bill—

The Second Wind can take us further than we would ever dare to imagine. God is a God of unlimited vision, and some of what he sees has our name written on it. He seems to specialize in doing amazing feats.

Astronauts have repeatedly commented about how marvelous it is to view our planet from space. No national borders, no fences, no barricades— just whole continents of green and tan and a little snow, with blue oceans alongside them, and all of it hanging like a jewel in the black sky. This is, of course, the view from where God sits as well. He is the ultimate big-picture person. He knows about petty constraints, but he doesn't pay a lot of attention to them. He is too busy jumping over our limitations and making more of our lives than any of us would predict.

A few years ago at a speakers' convention, I got acquainted with one of the best in the field, a lanky six-foot-six African American named Keith Harrell. He absolutely amazes audiences wherever he goes. His keynote speech, "Attitude Is Everything," commands impressive five-figure fees from Fortune 500 companies. His career really took off after the *Wall Street Journal* ran a major article on him back in March 1999. They even included five photos of him in action—a rare splash in the normally staid *Journal.*

The reporter included a quotation from Mark French, a booking agent: "There are over 4,000 professional speakers. Most of them are starving. There are a couple hundred who are doing well. There are probably 20 who are doing exceptionally well. Keith Harrell is doing exceptionally well."

What caught my attention during his speech was when he, right in the middle of talking about motivation, dropped the comment that he has a

Chuck Swindoll poster in his bathroom at home that he reads every morning. I used to work for Chuck Swindoll, so I wanted to find out more about Keith's spiritual foundation. We got together for a meal.

Come to find out, he grew up with a *serious* stuttering problem! This wildly successful public speaker today once suffered painful humiliation as a boy in Seattle trying to put words together.

"My mother would always say to me, 'Keith, your brain is moving faster than your mouth!'" he recalled. "Then she would add, 'Slow down; take your time.' That was fine until the first day of kindergarten came along. I can still remember the teacher asking me to stand and give my name. No words would come out. I couldn't get enough air.

"Instead, all I could hear was the other kids giggling and making fun."

Speech therapy helped somewhat, but all through Keith's grade-school years, he battled to communicate. "My classmates got to the point that when it was time to read out loud, they would volunteer me to go first. 'Pick Keith! Pick Keith!' they'd yell excitedly. They did this for two reasons.

"First, they knew I was too stubborn to quit. I'd stand up there all day if that's how long it took to read the passage.

"And that's the second reason…it took all day. They knew that if I was chosen to read out loud, no one else would have to read that day. I would eat up the entire period trying to plod through the material."

Keith's church experience was just as bad. When his mom would drop him off at the AME church for Sunday school, he would go in the front door and quickly head out the back, avoiding his class for fear of having to say something. After an hour of hanging out in a store or walking around the neighborhood, he would return to be picked up by his mother.

The fact that Keith eventually overcame his stuttering at the beginning of junior high and became fluent was due to his family's support and the hard work of his speech therapists, plus personal determination. But there is more to it than that, he says today. When in 2000 he was inducted into the Speakers Hall of Fame, he told the black-tie audience that night in Washington, D.C., "I'd like to give all the praise, all the glory and all the honor to my Lord and Savior, Jesus Christ. Through him all things are possible."

He is not worried in the least about how this kind of talk might affect his business with America's corporations. "My faith is my life," he says. "It's the rock on which I stand. It's everything to me. It's my source of inspiration. It's my source of motivation. It's my source of growth. It's my source of peace."

STOP RESISTING AND TURN GOD LOOSE

When God decides to propel a person into a whole greater dimension, he sometimes announces his intention in advance—as he did with Zechariah. But other times, he keeps his plans to himself, as with Keith Harrell. He stays quiet about what he has in mind.

Either way, his purposes prevail. And in the end, he receives the credit. Zechariah spoke boldly to everyone at his house that day:

Praise be to the Lord, the God of Israel,
  because he has come to his people and redeemed them.
He has raised up a horn of salvation for us
  in the house of his servant David
(as he said through his holy prophets of long ago),
salvation from our enemies
  and from the hand of all who hate us—
to show mercy to our ancestors
  and to remember his holy covenant,

the oath he swore to our father Abraham:
to rescue us from the hand of our enemies,
and to enable us to serve him without fear
in holiness and righteousness before him all our days.
(Luke 1:68-75)

Not much stuttering there! With eloquence inspired by the Holy Spirit, this overjoyed father described what God has done. The man who had been unable to speak for nearly a year suddenly gushed with praise and adoration of the Lord who does things beyond our comprehension.

The best thing we can do to foster God's action in our lives is to stop resisting or second-guessing, like Zechariah, and turn him loose. E. Stanley Jones, the notable Methodist missionary to India in the first half of the twentieth century, wrote about the meaning of surrender: "Just as the canvas surrenders itself to the painter, the violin to the musician, the wire to the electricity, so you put yourself at the disposal of the Divine. You surrender for better or for worse, for riches or for poverty, in sickness and in health, in life and in death—you will keep yourself only unto Him. He *has* you.

"Are you thereby lost, or thereby found? You are lost just as the musician is, when he takes the violin, surrenders himself to the music, lets go.... He is lost only to find himself a part of the universal harmony.... You die, just as an engine [locomotive] dies to the thought and purpose of wandering free anywhere and surrenders itself to the bondage of the rails—only to find its freedom there."[1]

To what amazing destinations might God take you if he had your full cooperation? Try it and see.

PERSONAL JOURNAL

- Can you imagine what it must have been like for Zechariah and Elizabeth to discover they were going to be parents at such a late stage of their life? What wild scenario have you had in your life that could in some way be called amazing?

_____

_____

_____

_____

_____

- Spend some time reading Luke 1 and 3. To give the text a fresh feel, try reading those chapters in a different translation or paraphrase, just as we did with the book of Jonah. This exercise should add some new levels of understanding to a fairly well-known text.

- What are some of your wildest dreams? List a few. Do you believe God can fulfill them? If not, what causes you to doubt? How can you overcome these doubts?

My Wildest Dreams

_____

_____

_____

_____

_____

_____

- How would you personalize Keith Harrell's story? What is the "stuttering" in your life that is keeping you from becoming a world-class success? Can God take that barrier away from your life as he did for Keith and Zechariah and Elizabeth?

_____

_____

_____

_____

_____

_____

_____

- Write God a brief letter, sharing with him your hopes, your dreams, and your aspirations. Ask him for the power of his Second Wind to help you achieve them. (Be prepared for his answer!)
  Dear God:

_____

_____

_____

_____

_____

_____

_____

_____

_____

_____

Your loving child,

_____

• What is the most important truth you gleaned from this chapter?

_____

_____

_____

_____

_____

_____

• Based on what you read in this chapter, how can *you* get a Second Wind?

_____

_____

_____

_____

_____

_____

CHAPTER 12

LIFE IS NOT A SPELLING BEE

—Bill—

Did you like the spelling part of elementary school? Maybe so, maybe not, depending on whether you were good at the subject. Either way, you can remember like it was yesterday.

Each Monday our teacher would present us with twenty new words to learn. Wednesday was the pretest to see how well we were doing. As the week wore on, the tension built toward Friday—the big test. We all knew this was make-or-break time. There was no arguing about whether you'd spelled a word correctly or not. Whatever the dictionary said was authoritative, no further discussion allowed.

Then, once a month, the teacher would add something "fun" to our wonderful world: the spelling bee. The class was divided into two teams, lined up on opposite sides of the room. We stood there glaring at the opponents across the way. Whose team would have the last person standing?

If the word was *cabbage,* you took a deep breath, began by repeating the word, and then started to spell: "C-A-B-B-A-G-E." You finished by saying the word once again.

It felt so good to get it right! But of course, if you weren't a good speller, the spelling bee was sheer torture. The teacher would lean over her desk and sternly say, "William, your word is *cabbage.*"

I'd swallow hard, break into a sweat, and mumble, "Cabbage. C-A-B-A-G-E. Cabbage."

"No, William, I'm afraid that is not correct. You may sit down."

The ultimate humiliation. As I'd shuffle toward my seat, my teammates would groan, and our opponents would snicker. I'd desperately want to plead with the teacher for another chance. But I knew it would do no good. Alas, the rules of the spelling bee were unyielding. Justice had to prevail.

Too Late?

As we grow into adulthood, many of us conclude that life is like grade-school spelling. One mistake and you're out.

But I have good news, my friend. Life is NOT a spelling bee. We've all made our share of mistakes, some more than others. But God will never ask any of us to sit down.

Some of us who thought life was a spelling bee now know differently. But we're still tempted to say, "I wish I had figured this out earlier. So much of my life has passed by."

Well, I have more good news: *It's never too late to get the words right.*

Think back on some of the biblical characters we've studied in this book.

- Moses was benched for forty years before God showed up one day and said, "Get back in the game, old fellow. I have a star role for you to play."
- Joshua had to bail out the Gibeonites whom he had stupidly promised to protect. After that fiasco, however, he went on to win a slew of future battles, eventually conquering the entire land of Canaan for God's people.

- Jonah rebounded from his deep-sea discipline with a stunningly successful preaching expedition to Nineveh.
- The cripple at the Pool of Bethesda—another man who was sidelined for nearly forty years—got up and ran off to a new life of freedom and excitement.
- The woman caught in adultery not only avoided a stoning from the Pharisees but was positioned to start a moral, respectable life.
- The believers in the Upper Room shook off their timidity and went out to turn the Roman Empire upside down with the good news of the risen Christ.
- The elderly Zechariah and Elizabeth became parents at last—parents of a future nation shaker.

This recurring theme throughout the biblical record gives us a huge dose of hope. God is on our side! He doesn't demand that we get it right the first time. He's willing to work with us, to coach us, to empower us, to breathe new energy into our faltering attempts. It doesn't matter how long it takes; he's got all the time in the world. He never gets to the point of saying with exasperation, "You know, just forget it." As long as we are open and teachable, "he who began a good work in you will carry it on to completion until the day of Christ Jesus" (Philippians 1:6).

BACK FROM THE CRASH

I've learned that truth in my own experience. As I told you in the first chapter of this book, I've known the pain of a marital disaster. My marriage of seventeen years ended in divorce in the spring of 1993, something that I wrote about in my earlier book *When Life Doesn't Turn Out Like You Planned*. My world came crashing down. I didn't know if I could endure the pain. I remember feeling completely drained of energy, both physically and emotionally. I dragged around the house like a blob of blubber—while trying to raise five kids.

Here's how I described it later in Focus on the Family's *Single-Parent Family* magazine:

> Some of my friends compared their divorces to being shot in the gut with a pistol. Mine felt like a one-two assault from a double-barreled shotgun. Not only was I blown away by the loss of the most treasured human relationship I had experienced, but the second shot blew me apart vocationally. Few groups wanted someone who was divorced to speak on marriages. Suddenly, I felt like a Lexus dealer driving a Dodge Dart.
>
> I did not work for six months. My debt grew every day. I felt I was no good to anybody....
>
> *No one is going to know my pain or embarrassment,* I concluded. *I will go under cover.* I became adept at dodging questions, avoiding eye contact and changing the subject. I was desperately lonely, deeply depressed and committed to a classic case of denial. I lived each day waiting for the phone to ring, hoping my wife would say she wanted to get back together.
>
> That call never came.[1]

Most significantly, I was listening to a small voice inside of me that was saying two things: "God could never use you again," and "You could never be loved by another."

I wrestled with those nagging thoughts for years. Friends were helpful. A fine counselor helped me sort out what had gone wrong, what was my fault, and what wasn't. Time brought new perspectives and some healing. My kids kept growing up, survived my cooking, and actually turned out better than you might have predicted.

But I still felt shelved.

One day Bill Hybels, my friend and the senior pastor of Willow Creek Community Church outside Chicago, called to invite me to speak at an event he was putting together.

I was shocked and a little embarrassed. "Thanks for the offer, Bill," I said. "But I don't think you know what's been going on in my life."

"Actually, I know *exactly* what's going on in your life," he replied. "That's why I called you. I want you to tell your story."

I remember wondering whether God might actually use me to encourage someone else who was struggling. I told Bill I'd give it a try.

As I finished my remarks that day, I was so utterly drained that I asked Bill to return to the podium and conclude the session instead of my trying to do it. He asked everyone to stand. He then instructed the people to encircle anyone in the room who they knew was in some kind of pain, while he led in prayer. There were circles everywhere!

That was the beginning. Word spread that maybe I had something to say after all. Promise Keepers asked me to speak at six of their upcoming stadium events. Other churches followed suit.

What was all of this? *A Second Wind.*

But there was the other part of that inner message that still haunted me. Could I ever be loved again?

I had regular conversations with God about this. He seemed to say, "Bill, am I enough for you?"

"What does that mean?" I would counter.

"You know I tell you in my Word that I will supply all your needs. Do you trust me enough to do that?"

"Well…," I would stammer.

"All your needs…even if it means remaining single for the rest of your life."

That was the lesson God wanted me to learn. All I needed was him.

I'm a slow learner; it took me seven years to get it. Finally I remember saying to the Lord, "If you want me single for the rest of my life, it's okay. I accept it. You are all I need."

Soon after that conversation in January 1999, I was invited to speak at an event at Mariners Church in Newport Beach, California. It was a Friday night kickoff for a small-group leaders retreat. After some introductions and a funny skit, I was handed the clip-on microphone by the one who had played the role of the skit's "straight man"—only in this case the straight man was a beautiful woman. There was no ring on her left hand.

I don't remember much about speaking that night. I am told I did a good job—who knows for sure? What I do remember is introducing myself to Kathi at the end of the evening. We conversed for only a few minutes, but I quietly sensed she was more than just a pretty face. She loved the Lord and had a depth to her character.

Not long after, we had our first date. We kept seeing each other, knowing that God was working in our lives. We grew in love. In September of that year we were married.

Please don't misunderstand. In no way am I trying to suggest that the answer to a struggling first marriage is a second marriage. Don't go chasing that fantasy. All I'm illustrating by telling you the facts about myself is that there seem to be circumstances when God, in his abundant grace, chooses to offer you a new dawn.

He's on Your Side

God has a Second Wind for you, too. If you're stuck in your career...if you're tormented by the wrongs done to you in the past...if you've messed up a marriage...if you've made any kind of unwise decision, God is not discouraged in the least. He's not wanting to discard you, to sweep you aside so he can concentrate on the smarter folks who've done everything right. He knows, in fact, that none of his creation is perfect, and working with fallible human beings is his only option.

We've shown you in this book how his Second Wind comes to different people in different ways. Your experience may look like someone's life you've read about in the Scriptures. It may look like one of the current examples we've recounted for you. Or it may be completely different from anything we've written.

As Moses said at the end of his run: "Be strong and courageous. Do not be afraid or terrified because of them, for the LORD your God goes with you; he will never leave you nor forsake you" (Deuteronomy 31:6).

God's Second Wind is there for you. He's promised.

Personal Journal

- Have you ever felt that life is like a spelling bee? How has that thought robbed you of energy? What other factors have drained you of your life?

  _____

  _____

  _____

  _____

  _____

  _____

- Page back over the past lessons of your journal. Which of the stories from Scripture was most significant to you? Why? What did you learn that was new? What came through in a fresh way?

  _____

  _____

  _____

  _____

  _____

  _____

  _____

- Which one of the current examples spoke most deeply to you? Why? How was it similar to your life story?

  _____

  _____

  _____

_____

_____

_____

- What will you do to keep the truths of this book alive in your life? Write out a little plan that will help you keep your goals.

_____

_____

_____

_____

_____

_____

- Will you continue a Second Wind journal? Will you commit to continue your Second Wind small group?

_____

_____

_____

_____

_____

- What is the most significant truth you gleaned from this entire book?

_____

_____

_____

_____

_____

_____

_____

- Based on what you read, list some of the ways you will make yourself available to the Second Wind.

  _____

  _____

  _____

  _____

  _____

  _____

  _____

GROUP STUDY GUIDE

Chapter 1: Huffing Toward Forty-Fourth Street

1. Go around the room and introduce yourselves to one another. We're going to be asking God for a Second Wind here together, so the more comfortable we are with each other, the more effective our group will be. Try some of these topics in order to get acquainted:

2. Bill's story of jogging on the beach may remind you of *your* favorite running story. It may be funny. It may be dramatic. It may be a bit embarrassing. It may be a personal triumph. Share it with the group.

3. Do you identify with the DMV employee? Does his job illustrate a life that has ground to a halt? Why does he need a Second Wind?

4. Can you relate to the single mom in this chapter? Has life turned out differently than you expected? How did you feel when she opened her Bible and couldn't find the encouragement she needed?

5. Have you had an experience in life that's a bit more dramatic, like the fellow who lost his job? How have you been able to make sense of these circumstances in your life?

6. Go around the room and complete the following sentence: "I am hoping that the promise of the Second Wind is for *me*. A Second Wind would be good right now because…"

7. Have someone in the group read aloud Psalm 42. Close your first session in prayer, asking God for the renewing and restoring that he promises in his Word. Ask him for a Second Wind.

Chapter 2: In the Midst of the Ordinary

1. Do you know anyone who has made a career change like Charlie's? Share with the group this person's story, including the fears and the triumphs.

2. Share with the group a personal anecdote that would describe you at your most "ordinary." Do you view an ordinary life of routine as a good thing or a bad thing? Why?

3. We looked at a slice of Moses' life we could describe as forty years of same-old same-old. Can you identify with this slice? Or is it a foreign concept to your personal experience? Share with the group as much as you are comfortable.

4. What's the closest thing to a modern-day burning bush that you've ever heard of? What's the closest thing *you* have ever personally experienced?

5. Have someone in the group read aloud James 1:17. What does this verse say to you about God's plan for your life?

6. Summarize this chapter in your own words. Perhaps you can begin with this sentence: "The promise of the Second Wind can occur in the midst of the ordinary. To me, this means…"

7. Based on what you read in this chapter, how can *you* get a Second Wind?

Chapter 3: Damaged Goods

1. Do you know anyone with a story similar to John Hesler's? Share it with the group. What about this story makes you uncomfortable? angry? sad? What in this story offers hope? Where is God's hand in all of this?

2. John reflected that Psalm 23:4 was a comfort to him: "Even though I walk through the valley of the shadow of death, I will fear no evil, for you are with me." It is such a familiar verse to many of

us. What does that verse mean to you? Does it take on new meaning as a result of reading this chapter?

3. First Peter 5:10 tells us we will suffer. (Have someone read it aloud.) So how do we deal with the damage done in our lives?

4. How does trauma prepare us for a Second Wind?

5. In your journal you reflected on how damaged men and women can be restored. Share with the group your thoughts and insights from that exercise.

6. Summarize this chapter in your own words. Perhaps you can begin with this sentence: "The promise of the Second Wind is available to those who've been traumatized. To me, this means…"

7. Based on what you read in this chapter, how can *you* get a Second Wind?

Chapter 4: Who's in Control?

1. Let's begin by having a few people in the group retell the story of Sandy Bolte. Start by sharing the factual side of her story, and then open it up to your own opinions, thoughts, and feelings.

2. This chapter includes this sentence: "When we surrender control of our lives to God, it frees him to let the Second Wind blow." Share with the group what that sentence means to you. Be as open and honest as possible.

3. Tell the group a little bit of your own personal story of control. Have you lived life "out of control"? Have you lived life under your own control? Have you lived life under God's control?

4. The lesson we learned from Joshua's life is to stand aside and let the Lord lead. What makes that concept so difficult? What are the roadblocks we experience to giving him control? What are the rewards of yielding to him?

5. Have someone in the group read aloud Jeremiah 29:11 (or better still, quote it together from memory). What stands out to you about the teaching of that verse?

6. Summarize this chapter in your own words. Perhaps you can begin with this sentence: "The promise of the Second Wind can occur when we settle the issue of who's in control of our lives. To me, this means…"

7. Based on what you read in this chapter, how can *you* get a Second Wind?

Chapter 5: Eligible for Good Things

1. Begin by sharing a humorous story, perhaps from your childhood, where you did *not* make the right decision and ended up paying the consequences.

2. On a more serious note, why is it difficult to make the right choices in life? Is it about integrity? Is it about peer pressure? Is it about the need to be loved and accepted? Is it something else?

3. Based on your rereading of Jonah in your personal time, share with the group one or two insights you saw afresh in that Old Testament book. Explain why they are meaningful to you.

4. Do you know a couple like Nelson and Judy Padgett? Share similar experiences with the group. Summarize your thoughts by finishing this sentence: "What makes their story so amazing is that…"

5. Has God ever spoken to you "a second time"? What was it like? Talk about God's love, God's grace, God's Second Wind.

6. Summarize this chapter in your own words. Perhaps you can begin with this sentence: "The promise of the Second Wind is available to those who make the right choices even when it's hard. To me, this means…"

7. Based on what you read in this chapter, how can *you* get a Second Wind?

Chapter 6: When It Can't Get Any Worse

1. Do you know anyone who has a story similar to Bill Freitag's? If so, share it with the group.

2. In the movie *City Slickers,* they played a game where they described their best day and then their worst day. Can you share with the group your descriptions of both of those days in your life?

3. One sentence in this chapter says, "Those who are at the absolute bottom of their lives, drained of all hope and promise, are still eligible for a merciful God to intervene." What does that sentence mean to you at your deepest, most personal level?

4. As you interacted with the account of the man at the pool, what caught your attention as most significant to the story? Is there anything in this text you had not seen before? What was it?

5. In your journal you reflected on what would keep you from going for a Second Wind in your life. Share with the group how fear plays into this scenario.

6. Summarize this chapter in your own words. Perhaps you can begin with this sentence: "The promise of the Second Wind can occur when life can't get any worse. To me, this means…"

7. Based on what you read in this chapter, how can *you* get a Second Wind?

Chapter 7: Facing Giants

1. Besides David versus Goliath (and Bill's little buddy at the Orange Bowl), what are some of your favorite stories of someone's facing a giant in his or her life and coming out victorious?

2. Did you relate to Don and Kay Bennett's story? What parts? If you didn't relate directly, what could it symbolize in your life?

3. What does it mean to you to be courageous? Be as practical with a definition as you can.

4. What does it mean to you to be proactive? Are you the kind of person who needs extra encouragement in order to take initiative, or are you someone who does it naturally? How does proactivity relate to our dependence on the Lord and his working in our lives?

5. Has God asked you to do something for him in your life? In this chapter we asked, "What is your *specific* calling here on earth?" How would you answer that question? If you don't know, how will you find out? If you do know the answer, what are you doing about it?

6. Summarize this chapter in your own words. Perhaps you can begin with this sentence: "The promise of the Second Wind is available to those who are proactive. To me, this means…"

7. Based on what you read in this chapter, how can *you* get a Second Wind?

Chapter 8: Yes, It Hurts

1. Have you ever had a medical experience that was considered life-or-death? Share with the group your most amazing medical miracle.

2. Based on what you studied in this chapter, discuss this major theological issue: Why does a loving God allow pain and suffering to enter our lives?

3. What's the difference among a trial, a test, and a temptation?

4. How would you explain the concept of firstfruits? What does that term add to our understanding of pain in our lives? Is there a

personal application you can make with something current in your life?

5. How can a Second Wind be born out of pain?

6. Summarize this chapter in your own words. Perhaps you can begin with this sentence: "The promise of the Second Wind is available to those who must endure pain. To me, this means…"

7. Based on what you read in this chapter, how can *you* get a Second Wind?

Chapter 9: Crying Out for Love

1. Okay, this could get interesting. What's something wild and crazy that happened to you in your college days (that you don't mind sharing with the group)?

2. On a more serious note, what churns inside of you when you hear the words "crying out for love"? These words could touch on some very personal pain, so be sensitive and supportive to your fellow group members as they share.

3. How did you feel as you were reading Amy Robnik's story? Did she remind you of yourself in those years? a son or daughter of yours? a close friend? Why do you think so many of us have stories like hers from that time in our lives?

4. In your journal you reflected on the thought "The craziness of the past does not have to dictate the future. We can learn to think in new ways according to God's truth." Share with the group some of your reflections.

5. Have someone in the group read aloud 2 Timothy 2:13. What does that verse teach us about God's character? What does that verse teach us about being in God's family? What does that verse teach us about the availability of God's Second Wind?

6. Summarize this chapter in your own words. Perhaps you can begin with the sentence: "The promise of the Second Wind is available to those crying out for love. To me, this means…"

7. Based on what you read in this chapter, how can *you* get a Second Wind?

Chapter 10: Wait a Minute

1. Most people have a story about themselves or a friend who was destined for pro sports, but something happened along the way to change the plan. Start your session with stories of people who almost went pro and why it didn't work out.

2. What's the most difficult experience you've ever had that involved waiting? How about when you were a child? a teenager? a young adult?

3. Why is waiting so hard? How does God use waiting in our lives? What are some lessons you've learned from waiting that can help you learn to wait today?

4. Suppose you were one of the apostles in Acts 1. Jesus had ascended, and you were left to wait. How would your story read? What would you have done? How would your account be similar to theirs? How would it be different?

5. What does it mean to you that the Greek word for *spirit* can also be translated *wind?* What's the connection in *your* life between the Holy Spirit and the Second Wind?

6. Summarize this chapter in your own words. Perhaps you can begin with this sentence: "The promise of the Second Wind is available to those who are forced to wait. To me, this means…"

7. Based on what you read in this chapter, how can *you* get a Second Wind?

Chapter 11: Beyond Our Wildest Dreams

1. Do you know anyone who wanted to have a baby but gave up hope only to become pregnant later in life? Share their story with the group. How did the couple feel about this event? Where did they see God in their circumstances?

2. Do you know someone with a story similar to Keith Harrell's? What did he or she have to overcome in order to live a life beyond his or her wildest dreams?

3. What are some of *your* wildest dreams? Are you open enough to share them with your group?

4. What have you learned in this study that offers you the hope that some of these dreams may come true? What still lingers inside of you that causes you to doubt?

5. How does the power of the Second Wind relate to dreams coming true? What does God want for you in your life? What did he tell Zechariah and Elizabeth that can encourage you right now?

6. Summarize this chapter in your own words. Perhaps you can begin with this sentence: "The promise of the Second Wind is available to those who want life beyond their wildest dreams. To me, this means…"

7. Based on what you read in this chapter, how can *you* get a Second Wind?

Chapter 12: Life Is Not a Spelling Bee

1. Have someone in the group make a list of all the biblical stories we looked at as well as the contemporary ones. Read each list aloud, then go around the room, with each person making one comment about each story. No other rules, just the first thing that comes to mind.

2. What was your favorite biblical account that we looked at? Why was it significant to you?

3. Which modern-day example was most meaningful to you? Why?

4. What is the most important lesson you learned from reading this book? from working in your journal? from meeting together with this small group?

5. Discuss ways to keep the message of the Second Wind plugged into your life now that the study is over.

6. How might this small group keep going? Is it meeting a need in your life that should be continued?

7. Summarize the message of the book in your own words. Perhaps you can begin with this sentence: "The promise of the Second Wind is available to *me*. It is *never* too late. To me, this means…"

NOTES

"On Risk"

1. Copyright © by Howard R. Macy, *Rhythms of the Inner Life: Yearning for Closeness with God* (Colorado Springs: Chariot Victor, 1999), 36-7. Copied with permission by Cook Communications Ministries. May not be further reproduced. All rights reserved.

"On Forgiveness"

1. Matthew Henry, *Matthew Henry's Commentary on the Whole Bible,* vol. 5, *Matthew to John,* commentary on Matthew 18. Found at www.ccel.org/h/henry/mhc2/MHC40018.

"On the Necessity of Coming Clean"

1. Patrick Kavanaugh, *Spiritual Moments with the Great Composers: Daily Devotions form the Lives of Favorite Composers & Hymn Writers* (Grand Rapids: Zondervan, 1995), 135-6.

"On Coping with the Unfairness of Others"

1. Thomas à Kempis, *The Imitation of Christ,* trans. E. M. Blaiklock (Nashville: Nelson, 1981), 40-1.

"On Surrender and Faith"

1. Hannah Whitall Smith, *The Christian's Secret of a Happy Life* (New York: Revell, 1941), 46-56.

"On Overcoming"

1. Dwight L. Moody, *A Treasury of Dwight L. Moody*, ed. Ralph G. Turnbull (Grand Rapids: Baker, 1971), 30-7.

"On Pain and Its Purposes"

1. E. Stanley Jones, *Abundant Living* (New York: Abingdon, 1942), 277-9, 281.

"On Coming Back to God's Favor"

1. John Wesley, *The Works of John Wesley*, 3d ed., vol. 6 (London: Wesley Methodist Book Room, 1872), 525-7.

"On Grace"

1. Charles H. Spurgeon, *Spurgeon at His Best: Over 2200 Striking Quotations from the World's Most Exhaustive and Widely-Read Sermon Series*, comp. Tom Carter (Grand Rapids: Baker, 1988), 86-90.

Chapter 11: Beyond Our Wildest Dreams

1. Jones, *Abundant Living*, 157.

Chapter 12: Life Is Not a Spelling Bee

1. Bill Butterworth, "When You're Forced to Regroup," *Single-Parent Family* 3, no. 1 (January 1996): 15.

ABOUT THE AUTHORS

Bill Butterworth is an award-winning communicator whose talks, tapes, columns, and books are providing education and encouragement to businesspeople throughout North America. Through the wit, warmth, insight, and realism of his presentations, he brings help and hope to his audiences everywhere.

Bill taught at the college level for thirteen years and was a counselor for six years prior to his current passion for motivating men and women in the workplace through speaking and writing.

In the writing world, Bill has established himself as a successful talent with a wide variety of accomplishments. He has written more than a dozen books, both under his own name and as a ghostwriter, ranging from psychology, to self-help issues, to one of his favorite releases, the autobiography of one of football's Dallas Cowboys. He has been a columnist, an editor, and a scriptwriter for Warner Brothers.

Bill maintains a heavy speaking schedule at conventions, conferences, retreats, banquets, businesses, churches, and school-sponsored lectures. Not only has he been warmly received at such great churches as Willow Creek Community Church and Saddleback Community Church, he has also addressed such corporate clients as Disney, American Express, Daimler-Chrysler, Nortel, Bank of America, Verizon, Ford Motor Company, Young President's Organization, PNC Bank, Northwestern Mutual Insurance Company, Century 21 Real Estate, the American Trucking Association, SBC, the American Institute of Certified Public Accountants, and his favorite, twenty-six teams of the National Football League. With humor and engaging enthusiasm, Bill drives home points in an unforgettable way.